SONG WITHOUT WORDS

THE STORY OF FELIX MENDELSSOHN

Song Without Words

The Story of

Felix Mendelssohn

by John Erskine

Julian Messner, Inc.
New York

PUBLISHED BY JULIAN MESSNER, INC.
8 WEST 40TH STREET, NEW YORK

PRINTED IN THE UNITED STATES OF AMERICA
BY MONTAUK BOOK MANUFACTURING CORP., NEW YORK

2E

My thanks to Margaret Miller and to Oscar Wagner for reading proofs of this book. They did their best to take the errors out of it.

JOHN ERSKINE.

Contents

Introduction

AKOB LUDWIG FELIX MENDELSSOHN-Bartholdy was a wonder child of music. His life was short, but into it was crowded almost incredible accomplishment and the rarest of good fortune. The happiness which he enjoyed is held against him by some biographers, who suggest that he might have been a greater man, and his music might now seem to us more profound, if he had had his share of hard knocks. That point of view will not be found in this book.

The best of his fortune was his character, a direct gift from remarkable parents and grandparents. That he was rich and that he enjoyed extraordinary opportunities to improve himself, followed naturally from great intelligence and prodigious industry in his elders. His genius was the gift of heaven, but the history of art is full of geniuses who miss the success to which, as we say, they were entitled. He had genius, but he worked. If Felix Mendelssohn seemed properly named a happy child, we should remember that he and his sister Fanny were always glad when Sunday came, since on that day they didn't have to get up at five o'clock to study their lessons.

His grandfather, Moses Mendelssohn, was a famous philosopher. His father, an important banker, used to say with a laugh that he was only a hyphen between the first and the third generation. His mother, herself a musician, trained her four children, Fanny, Felix, Rebecca and Paul, to develop their gifts to the utmost, rebuking them firmly when they showed the slightest disposition, even in their earliest years, to dawdle or waste time. If her curly-haired, dark-eyed wonder child stood idle a moment after luncheon, listening perhaps to the talk of a famous visitor, she would say, "Felix, have you nothing to do?" and the child would get at his piano, or his violin, or his composing, or his landscape drawing, or his books. She herself gave Fanny and Felix their first piano lessons, and for years she sat beside them while they practiced, so that no measure should be played even once the wrong way.

With such discipline you might expect a genius to acquire some resentment toward his parents, but Felix adored both his father and his mother, and he loved his home. With good reason. The theory on which he was educated was nearly, if not quite, ideal. His curiosity was encouraged, and study was presented to him not as a blind routine, but always as a means of getting at something which otherwise would be inaccessible.

He began composing at an extremely early age. By the time he was thirteen he had written some sixty pieces for piano and violin, for string quartet, for voices, and for small orchestra. He had even composed three operettas, the texts of which had been furnished by an acquaintance of his father's, a physician, who exercised his bass voice, how well we don't know, but certainly with an amateur's relish. The habit of incessant composition remained with Felix all his life. Perhaps it exhausted him. He completed his wonderful oratorio "Elijah" only a short time before his death.

We think of him now chiefly as a composer whose music, even in his least important moments, is masterly and graceful, and at its best radiantly beautiful. Its spirit is always the spirit of song. In his lifetime he had a virtuoso's success at the piano and organ. Perhaps it is misleading to speak of him as a virtuoso. A contemporary of Liszt, he was thought by some critics to play as well or even better. The characteristic of his performances is said to have been that you forgot entirely the technique, and heard only the music. He was honored then, and gratefully remembered now, for something more. His judgment of the great composers before him is indorsed by modern opinion. The reason is that he helped shape modern opinion. Sebastian Bach, though understood by a few men like Mendelssohn's own composition teacher, Zelter, did not come into his own until Felix, at the age of twenty, gave the great "Passion" a public performance in Berlin. By his own concert work he established more firmly in the public esteem the profound sonatas and concertos of Beethoven, and against the taste of his contemporaries he insisted on the greatness of Beethoven's later sonatas and string quartets.

He visited England and made upon that country a deeper impression than any other composer, even Handel. Indeed, the English worship of him was so excessive as to react against his reputation in our time. In Great Britain to this day young ladies in the provinces take the bloom off an evening party by pious renderings of his more sentimental songs and duets. Grove's Dictionary, the standard English encyclopedia of music and musicians, assigned in its 1904 edition eight pages to Sebastian Bach and sixty-six to Felix Mendelssohn. If Felix heard of it in Heaven, he must have caused a scandal in the place, for he was an honest critic and a just man, and he inherited his father's quick temper.

Today his reputation rises again, and this little book will try to tell the reasons. That he was underrated in recent decades is an ironic commentary on human nature. How many children have wished their parents would understand them, and cease to obstruct? This boy's parents understood him perfectly and gave him precisely the life he desired. How many artists have groaned over lack of opportunity, or have described to us the masterpieces they would produce if someone would provide a little preliminary endowment? Felix had the preliminary endowment, and he produced the masterpieces. Human nature being what it is, he couldn't escape envy. Quite a number of artists, contemplating the clear record, have shaken their heads, and have feared that though angels may produce the best art out of beatitude, man cannot.

SONG WITHOUT WORDS

THE STORY OF FELIX MENDELSSOHN

CHAPTER ONE

Music in the Home

ON SUNDAY MORNING, ANY SUNDAY
morning, in the year 1822, there was a
remarkable gathering in the Mendelssohn house, in the Neue Promenade,
between the Spree and the Haacksche
Markt. If you happened to be a musician
of importance, or a real poet, or a
painter, a philosopher or a diplomat,
whether a resident of Berlin or a traveler
passing through, you would probably

receive an invitation, and you would cancel other engagements and go, even though you knew in advance that the chief performer was a child of thirteen.

The house belonged to Grandmother Mendelssohn, widow of the famous Moses, who had understood Plato and had expressed some ideas of his own about the universe. Grandfather Moses had improved on most philosophers by being wealthy, as you could see from this house. In furniture and decorations it was rather ostentatiously plain, but it had many books and a grand piano, and the few pictures on the walls were of the best.

The widow Mendelssohn did not live alone. With her resided her son Abraham, who had married Lea Salomon. Lea had an interesting brother in the diplomatic service who had taken to himself the name Bartholdy because he liked the sound of it, who adopted the Christian faith, and who at his death left his sister a fortune. Abraham had been living in Hamburg when Felix was born, but the Napoleonic wars rendered that city most unpleasant, and in 1811 Abraham took his family to Berlin to his mother's house.

He shared his brother-in-law's liking for the name Bartholdy, and added it to his own. He and Lea also joined the Christian church and had their children baptized. In this step they may have been following the liberal philosophy of Grandfather Moses, or they may have been influenced by the religious sentiment of the day, which in Protestant Germany remembered that Jesus was the supreme prophet of Hebrew wisdom and faith,

4

and thought it a tragedy of the first order that history had separated the Christians from the Jews. Heine too, we remember, was baptized into Christianity; so was Karl Marx. In later years they were not happy about it, but those remarkable Mendelssohns remained content with both the Old Testament and the New, profoundly religious, bothered as little as possible by the differences which usually keep religious folk apart. Felix was at home in the Jewish temple, in the Protestant chapel, and in the Catholic church, to which some relatives of his belonged. But he was glad of the concerts which his father arranged on Sunday mornings.

Had we been among the fortunate guests at one of those musical parties, we should have been ushered into the large dining room, and unless we came late, we could slip into a seat near the door. Grandmother Mendelssohn liked to have chairs for her guests, but if too many appeared, as sometimes happened, they just had to stand.

Around the large table was gathered a decidedly mixed company, young men and women, several older men, all with sheets of music laid out before them. From the way they handled the pages and from their laughing remarks, you would gather that none of them had seen the music before, and those who feared they couldn't read the manuscript, miraculously neat though it was, were probably amateurs. Beyond the table stood the grand piano, placed in the dining room because, except during meals, the dining room was the family concert hall. At the piano presided, more likely than not, Fanny Mendelssohn, a bril-

5

liant player though only seventeen years old. Around the piano were grouped a small orchestra, players from the Court band hired for these Sunday concerts by Felix's father. Seated with these musicians, but warned by his brother not to do any harm, was nine-year-old Paul, who was learning the 'cello.

At the head of the table, at a conductor's desk, where singers, orchestra, and pianist could see him, stood Felix, on a helpful box or stool. He wore a tight-fitting, low-necked jacket, over which wide trousers were buttoned. Evidently he had been advised to break the habit of sticking one hand into a pocket, making the wide trouser balloon out. In ordinary conversation, when he looked up at you, he stuck both hands in, and the trousers ballooned symmetrically. He wore long brown curls. When he spoke he lisped slightly, and he had a nervous habit of shifting from one foot to the other.

This morning his father had encouraged him to try out his one-act opera *Die beiden Pädagogen* (The Two School Teachers). These leading characters were bass parts, and at one point they sang a duet. Doctor Caspar, who had written the libretto, was on hand with his enthusiastic voice, very bass and very amateurish. Next him at the table sat a young professional baritone, Eduard Devrient, a fine singer and excellent musician, who already looked up to the thirteen-year-old Felix as to a mature colleague, and whose recollections of Mendelssohn, written and published years afterwards, give us the account of this scene.

6

At these Sunday morning concerts you would be sure to see Felix's teacher of harmony and counterpoint, Carl Friedrich Zelter, a strong and healthy-looking gentleman of sixty years or more, good-hearted but a born critic, ready to pounce on a mistake. He had elements of greatness, and his influence on his pupil deserves our attention. In his youth he had set to music some of Goethe's lyrics, which is not always a good way to win a poet's esteem, but Goethe became his life-long friend, and through Zelter the author of *Faust* and Felix were to know each other well.

Zelter served the boy even better by admitting him to the *Singakademie* and introducing him to the music of Sebastian Bach. The *Singakademie* was a small group of excellent singers devoted to the study of choral music, accompanied and unaccompanied. The society had been founded in 1790 by Carl Friedrich Christian Fasch, and from 1792 to 1800 Zelter was the accompanist, after 1800 succeeding Fasch as director. Fasch, a devoted pupil of Sebastian Bach's, passed on his enthusiasm to Zelter, and under them both the *Singakademie* studied some of Bach's work, in a day when musicians in general did not yet appreciate it. To his early experience with this music, almost as much as to Zelter's excellent instruction, Felix owed the soundness and the facility of his contrapuntal writing. But in one conviction he differed with his teacher. Zelter thought Bach needed editing and abbreviating; Felix thought the great master could be trusted to speak for himself.

Now at the Sunday concerts Zelter listened for slips in counterpoint or harmony, for questionable use of the voices, for weak scoring of the instruments. He had to listen hard. The boy's musical ideas might be immature, but he was already a good craftsman.

At the first lift of the baton you could see that the technique of conducting was second nature to him. He played on the little orchestra as easily as on his piano. Fortunately he lacked the show-off tendency which makes some elder conductors ridiculous. Nothing could surpass the sincerity with which he brought out the qualities of his graceful music, listening intently to the effects in which he was experimenting, with meticulous care giving the voices as well as the instruments their cues, stopping only when it was necessary, and suggesting with precision the better way to perform the passage.

His earnestness and his sincerity did not conceal his high spirits or his quick sense of humor. As much as anyone in the room he enjoyed the bass duet, sung by the Doctor *con amore* and by Devrient correctly. The spirit of play, as the guests remarked, could be felt in everything the Mendelssohns did. That family had the joy of life.

At the close of the performance there was applause, of course, which Felix did not acknowledge; he joined in it as a tribute to players and singers. Criticism of the music he expected from Zelter, and he got it at once. Two or three points he was quick to anticipate, having seen during the performance what was wrong. Then his mother thought

8

they might enjoy some refreshments, as soon as Doctor Caspar and Herr Devrient should persuade each other how the duet ought really to be sung. The company pushed back their chairs. The singers left the dining table. Felix gathered up the vocal and instrumental parts, counting them to see that none was missing. He had copied them himself in his neat hand, a task which you and I would think formidable, but a small matter for a passionate composer who rose at five o'clock in the morning to get at his work.

CHAPTER TWO

Visits to Goethe

MENDELSSOHN'S BOYHOOD WAS EVI-
dently marked by such good fortune as
might easily have made him a spoiled
child. He enjoyed privileges most human
beings miss, and opportunities every
artist needs but usually doesn't get. An
artist needs, among other important
things, an audience. A composer, in particular, learns by hearing his music and
seeing its effect on other people. From

infancy, we might say, Mendelssohn found in his father's house an immediate audience, remarkable for its competence to criticize and help, and for its still rarer competence to avoid flattering him. He was not a spoiled child. Even as a boy he was unusually magnanimous, large-minded, large-souled.

Undoubtedly he had his character from his parents and from his remarkable grandfather, to dig no further into his ancestry, and beyond question his father's wealth gave him some good things he otherwise would have lacked, but it would be misleading to speak of his good fortune as though it were chiefly a matter of money. His best fortune was in the friends who encircled him from his earliest days. He grew up among great men, and those of his acquaintances who were not great were at least extraordinary. Friendship with any one of them would have stimulated his mind and guided his heart.

There was Zelter, his teacher, a composer, an all-around musician, singularly independent in thought and manners. Beginning life as a mason's apprentice, by force of talent and will he had taught himself music and reached distinction in the art. Several lyrics of Goethe's he had set to music, and the poet became his friend, a consequence which in such cases is not always inevitable. Goethe may have admired his personality more than his compositions. It was no bad thing for Mendelssohn, growing up in a cultured home, to know this self-made man, rugged and angular.

There was Ignace Moscheles, born in Prague in 1794,

himself an infant prodigy both as performer and composer. At a time when his reputation in Germany perhaps exceeded that of any other pianist, he frequented the Mendelssohn house in Berlin. For six weeks in November and December, 1824, he was a constant visitor. Felix's parents persuaded him to give the boy lessons every other day. No one has paid more enthusiastic tribute to the Mendelssohn family as a group, and his tribute to the boy, as he accepted the invitation to teach him, is often quoted: "He has no need of lessons. If he wishes to take a hint from me as to anything new to him, he can easily do so."

On a trip to Paris with his father in 1825, Mendelssohn saw much of Moscheles and became well acquainted with Johann Nepomuk Hummel, pianist and composer, Jacques Francois Halévy, composer, Frederik Wilhelm Kalkbrenner, pianist and composer, Gioacchino Antonio Rossini and Giacomo Meyerbeer, both famous chiefly as dramatic composers, and Mario Luigi Cherubini, composer of operas and church music. To say that all of these men, then or later, were Mendelssohn's friends would be not quite accurate. In his letters home he withheld his approval from some of them while admitting their kindness. He was already an ardent admirer of the best German music beginning with Bach, but German music had as yet made little impression on the Latin peoples, and he was disgusted with this French group for what he considered their ignorance. The criticism was boyish, but as we now feel, just. Yet whatever he thought of their taste in art, he knew their eminence in the world, and their acquaintance broadened his point of view. Old Cherubini, then the director of the Conservatoire, was the most outspoken in his recognition of the boy's genius, and Mendelssohn granted that the man had some of the qualities of a volcano, though extinct.

But the friend which we like to think counted most in shaping his character was Goethe, seventy-two years old and world-famous when Mendelssohn first visited him in 1821. Zelter arranged the meeting, and for sixteen days the young musician and the old poet enjoyed each other's society as equals, or as nearly equal as the difference in age would permit. There was a second visit to Weimar in 1822, when Mendelssohn stopped with his parents and his sister Fanny to pay his respects, and another short visit in 1825 on his return from Paris with his father and his aunt.

In the letter in which Zelter asked permission to bring his best pupil, he described the boy as good and good-looking, energetic and obedient. The description, though true enough, portrays Zelter more completely than Mendelssohn. The moral character is stressed, the genius is hardly mentioned. Perhaps there was no need to mention it. Goethe soon recognized the extraordinary gifts of his young visitor.

The Mendelssohn family were no little excited. Felix's mother wrote to his Aunt Henriette in Paris, "The lucky little rascal is going to Weimar." His father advised him not to forget his manners. Both his mother and his sister

Fanny begged him to write down everything Goethe said and did.

The famous visit is recorded in a little book called *Goethe and Mendelssohn,* written long afterwards by the composer's son, Karl, and translated by M. E. von Glehn. Some of the material upon which Karl Mendelssohn drew is contained also in the collection of *Letters and Journals of the Mendelssohn Family,* made by Sebastian Hensel, the son of Mendelssohn's sister, Fanny, and translated by Carl Klingemann. In the quotations which are given here, I shall use what seems the best of either translation.

Mendelssohn obeyed the family injunction to send frequent and full letters. Remember that he was only twelve years old at the time, had composed two operas or operettas, and was working on a third, had written six symphonies, a quartet for piano and strings, a cantata, six fugues for piano, besides songs, sonatas, and innumerable smaller matters!

On Tuesday, November 6, 1821, he describes the previous Sunday, the day on which he met Goethe. Zelter had taken him to church in the morning to hear Handel's setting of the One-hundredth Psalm, and before speaking of the poet, the boy gives his opinion that the Weimar organ, though large, is weak. For the information of his father's household he adds that the Weimar organ has fifty stops, forty-four notes, and one thirty-two-foot pipe.

Then he passes on to Goethe, first seen in the garden coming around a hedge, and Mendelssohn remarks on

14

the circumstance that he had heard his father describe *his* meeting with Goethe exactly in the same way.

"He is very kind," the letter goes on, "but I don't think any of his portraits resemble him. He looked over his collection of fossils which his son had arranged for him, and kept saying, 'Hm, Hm! I am very much pleased.' Then I walked in the garden with him and Professor Zelter for half an hour. Then came dinner. One would never take him for seventy-three, for fifty, rather. After dinner Fräulein Ulrike, the sister of Frau von Goethe, asked for a kiss, and I did the same. Every morning I get a kiss from the author of 'Faust' and 'Werther,' and every afternoon two kisses from my friend and father Goethe. Think of that! (In Leipzig I went several times through Auerbach's curious courtyard, a great passage, like many others in Leipzig, filled with shops and people, and shut in by houses six or seven stories high. In the market-place there is actually one of nine stories.)

"But where am I wandering to! After dinner I played to Goethe for two hours and more, partly Bach fugues, and partly extempore."

He then tells Fanny that he took the manuscripts of some songs she had composed to Frau von Goethe, who had a good voice and would sing them to the poet.

On November 10th he writes, "Monday I went to see Frau von Henkel, and also his Royal Highness the Hereditary Grand Duke, who was very much pleased with my Sonata in G minor. On Wednesday evening a very pretty opera, 'Oberon,' by Wranitzky, was given. On Thursday

morning the Grand Duke, the Duchess, and the Hereditary Grand Duke came to us, and I had to play. And I
played from eleven in the morning till ten in the evening,
with only two hours' interruption, finishing with Hummel's Fantasia. When I was with him the other day, I
played the Sonata in G minor, which he liked very much,
also the piece for Begas, and yours, dear Fanny. I play
much more here than at home, seldom less than four
hours, and sometimes even eight. Every afternoon Goethe
opens his instrument (a Streicher) with the words, 'I have
not yet heard you today—now make a little noise for me.'
And then he generally sits down by my side, and when I
have done (mostly extemporising) I ask for a kiss, or I
take one. You cannot fancy how good and kind he is
to me, no more can you form an idea of the treasures in
minerals, busts, prints, statues, and large original drawings, etc., which the polar star of poets possesses. It does
not strike me that his figure is imposing; he is not much
taller than father; but his look, his language, his name,
they are imposing. The amount of sound in his voice is
wonderful, and he can shout like ten thousand warriors.
His hair is not yet white, his step is firm, his way of
speaking mild."

The boy appreciated to the full the rare privilege he
was enjoying, and it is clear that he stored up for life-long
remembrance every impression the poet then made on
him, but his hero-worship was discriminating; he seems
to have realized that Goethe was not a musician, and that
the old man's interest was in the phenomenon of genius

more than in the particular art in which the genius was displayed. On the first day of the visit and for several days afterward he quite obviously was putting the boy through his paces, trying to find the limitations of his gifts. The letters home indicate that Goethe was trying to stump him. He asked for an improvisation, and Felix improvised on a theme of Zelter's. He then called for Bach Preludes and Fugues. He then asked for some minuets.

"Shall I play the most beautiful one in the world?" said Mendelssohn, striking into the minuet from *Don Giovanni*.

Goethe then asked for an overture, and Mendelssohn played the overture to *Figaro*. It isn't clear whether Goethe was testing the boy's memory or whether he was sufficiently a musician to be interested in the piano version Mendelssohn promptly made. He then tested his ability to read by putting before him a Mozart manuscript, which Mendelssohn had no difficulty in playing at sight. Then for that day's climax Goethe brought out another manuscript, covered with blots and erasures, apparently a hopeless scrawl. Mendelssohn studied it for several minutes before he recognized Beethoven's notoriously bad script. Goethe teased him a little, suggesting that here his sight-reading ability ended, but after a little more study of the score, Mendelssohn played it with ease.

The old poet set up hurdles for him on later occasions, but the first test had convinced him that the boy was of the authentic elect.

A few days later some Weimar musicians were invited in to play Mendelssohn's first quartet, the B minor, Opus 3, which on a later visit he dedicated to Goethe. One of the players remembered what Goethe, after the performance, said to Zelter. "Musical prodigies so far as mere technique is concerned are no longer rare, but what this little fellow can do in extemporising and playing at sight is miraculous. I shouldn't have believed it possible in one so young."

"But you heard Mozart when he was seven years old," said Zelter.

"Yes," said Goethe. "I was then only twelve, and like everybody else was astonished at his extraordinary performance. But what your pupil has already accomplished is to the Mozart of that time as the conversation of an adult is to the talk of a child."

During the Weimar visit Felix was kept busy playing for all comers, from local musicians to visiting royalty. With the ease of manner which he had shown in Goethe's presence, he improvised before the Grand Duke and Duchess of Russia, and played for them his G minor Sonata, already mentioned in his letter of November 10th. This Sonata, begun June 18, 1820, and finished August 18, 1821, was published much later as Opus 105.

In February, 1822, in a letter to Zelter, Goethe sent affectionate greetings to Felix and his parents, and mourned the fact that since the boy had played on it, his piano had remained dumb. The remark seems to have led up to a second visit. In the autumn Felix stopped at

Weimar for a few days with his parents and his sister Fanny.

We have the statement of Felix's mother that his happy parents were proud to owe to him the wonderful kindness with which they were received. Goethe, she says, "is so sweet and kind-hearted, and so like a father to the boy, that it is only with the deepest gratitude and most joyful emotion that I can recall these delightful times. He talked for hours with my husband about Felix, and earnestly begged to have him again for a still longer visit; his eyes dwelt on him with evident satisfaction, and his gravity changed into gaiety when he had been improvising to his satisfaction. As he does not care for ordinary music, his piano had remained untouched during Felix's absence, but as he opened it for him he said, 'Come and awaken for me all the winged spirits which have so long been slumbering here.' And another time: 'You are my David, and if I am ever ill and sad, you must banish my bad dreams by your playing; I shall never throw my spear at you, as Saul did.' Isn't that too touching from an old man of seventy-three? Felix, who in a general way seems rather indifferent to praise, is, with good reason, proud of the favor which Goethe shows him, and this feeling can only elevate and improve him."

In 1825 on the return from Paris Felix stopped with his father and his Aunt Henriette for a third visit, played the B minor Quartet and dedicated it to the poet. Goethe acknowledged the honor in an affectionate letter, saying that the Quartet seems to him the embodiment of the rich energetic soul which at first acquaintance had so astonished him.

Mendelssohn's last visit to Goethe occurred in 1830, when he was twenty-one years old. By this time he had studied at the University of Berlin, had traveled widely, and had won his fame as composer and performer. He stopped at Weimar at the end of May, breaking a journey to Rome.

Goethe, he says, was unchanged in appearance, but somewhat silent in manner, even languid. To that extent old age had quenched a once inexhaustible enthusiasm, but after a little conversation the high spirits returned, particularly at the mention of various women's societies recently formed in Weimar, modern innovations of which Goethe did not approve. He made endless fun of charity bazaars, literary societies, and organized subscriptions for good works where the real purpose was social self-promotion. After that general blast he was himself again and exhibited nothing less than his full mental vigor for the remainder of Mendelssohn's stay.

Every morning Felix played to him, always putting the composers in historical order, and at Goethe's request commenting on the characteristics of each. During the playing the old poet sat in a shadowed corner looking like Jove himself. He was reluctant to admire Beethoven, but Mendelssohn played to him the first movement of the C minor Symphony until he conceded its quality, and remarked that if it sounded magnificent on a piano, what must it be if all the people were playing it at once!

By this time he had accepted Mendelssohn as one of the truly great, and as on the former visits he now asked distinguished folk to his house for some music, and when Felix played, his invariable comment was, *"Ganz stupend!"* (Simply stupendous!)

The best of this final visit, however, was his talk of his own youth. The impression on Mendelssohn was profound—the recollections of Schiller and of Jean Paul, of dead conservatism breaking down and a new creative age beginning. When he thanked Goethe for sharing those memories with him, the old man answered simply that they were called up by the charm of his visitor. Next morning he gave Felix a page of the manuscript of *Faust,* with this inscription: "To my dear young friend, F.M.B., strong and subtle master of the piano, to remind him of happy May days in 1830. J.W. v. Goethe."

We can recover precious things out of the remote past only by imagination and judicious guesswork, and all history is full of mistakes, but we may easily persuade ourselves that Goethe exerted upon Mendelssohn an influence almost as great as that of his parents. These visits made him familiar at the beginning of his life with one of the noblest spirits of any age. All his own good impulses, we think, must have been strengthened by acquaintance with the giant whose endless curiosity, whose passion for creation, and whose lofty ideals in art he could imitate and approach, but not surpass. The two exchanged letters for the short remainder of Goethe's life, but saw each other no more.

To complete the picture of this famous friendship we recall what Goethe said of this final visit, writing to Zelter: "His coming did me a great deal of good, for my feelings about music are unchanged; I hear it with pleasure, interest, and reflection; I love its history, for who can understand any subject without thoroughly initiating himself into its origin and progress? It is a great thing that Felix fully recognizes the value of going through its successive stages, and happily his memory is so good as to furnish him with any number of examples of all kinds. From the Bach period downwards he has brought Haydn, Mozart, and Gluck to life for me, has given me clear ideas of the great modern masters of technique, and lastly has made me understand his own productions, and left me plenty to think about in himself. He took away with him my warmest blessing."

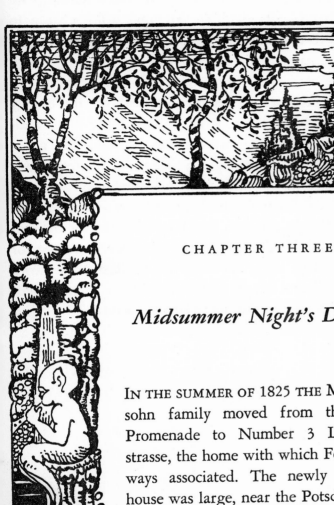

CHAPTER THREE

Midsummer Night's Dream

IN THE SUMMER OF 1825 THE MENDELS-
sohn family moved from the Neue
Promenade to Number 3 Leipzigerstrasse, the home with which Felix is always associated. The newly acquired
house was large, near the Potsdam Gate
in a part of Berlin then more country
than city. Besides the main building the
estate contained various offices or garden
houses, and a beautiful park of about

23

ten acres. In the main house there was a room large enough for concerts and plays, and one of the additional buildings could accommodate several hundred music lovers at once—that is, in summer; the building wasn't heated.

The removal to Number 3 Leipzigerstrasse marked an advance in Mendelssohn. Beyond doubt it coincided with a fresh current of musical inspiration which inevitably is associated with happy hours in the new home, especially in the delightful park. During the first year of residence Felix poured out an incredible amount of work, all mature and vital. Two of these compositions remain among the unforgettable things of music, the Octet in E flat for Strings (Op. 20), and the Overture to the *Midsummer Night's Dream*. The Octet was finished in 1825, at the end of the first summer in the new home. The *Midsummer Night's Dream* Overture was finished at the end of the following summer. They belong together in mood and inspiration, the Octet being a kind of preliminary study in certain orchestral effects for which the Overture is famous.

Felix told his sister Fanny that the Scherzo of the Octet was an attempt to restate in music a stanza from the Walpurgis-night Dream in *Faust.* The Overture was obviously a musical translation of the spirit of *Midsummer Night's Dream.* This complete transference to music of something which had already been expressed supremely in words was an accomplishment peculiar to Mendelssohn's genius. We shall have occasion to refer to it again.

A scherzo is a swift, light movement, faster than a minuet, and usually said to be developed out of that form, since Beethoven used it in his symphonies and sonatas to replace the stately dance. In mood, however, it is entirely different from the minuet. It is not strictly a dance at all, but a flight of mind or spirit, ranging from irony and lightning brilliance to the most ethereal poetic fancy. Mendelssohn's scherzos are of the poetic kind, and on the whole no composer has matched them in joyous unearthly beauty. So far do they depart from the minuet tradition that they rely for their effect on no one rhythm; the Scherzo of the Octet is written in 2-4 time. Fanny's description of it cannot be bettered: ". . . the whole piece is to be played staccato and pianissimo, the tremulandos coming in now and then, the trills passing away with the quickness of lightning; everything new and strange, and at the same time most insinuating and pleasing, one feels so near the world of spirits, carried away in the air, half inclined to snatch up a broomstick and follow the aerial procession. At the end the first violin takes a flight with a featherlike lightness, and—all has vanished."

The Finale of the Octet is a splendidly written fugue, but it is interesting for something more than its illustration of Mendelssohn's expert counterpoint. It uses the subject of the Scherzo, slightly changed, and is therefore an instance of what in later music is called cyclic form— the building up of a whole composition by repeating a theme or several themes, changed or developed as they recur. Or rather, the subject of the Finale is the counterpoint of the Scherzo subject so that they can both be played together. The theme of the Scherzo is—

The counterpoint in the Finale—

How well they fit we see if we superimpose them—

The Finale, in fact, is merely an extension of the Scherzo at a quicker tempo. Toward the end the Scherzo theme is reintroduced.

The Mendelssohn family threw themselves with their usual enthusiasm into the enjoyment of the new home, particularly of the park and the garden. During the summer of 1826 all four children, Felix, Fanny, Rebecca, and Paul, with companions of their own age, turned the afternoons and twilights into what has been described as an uninterrupted carnival of poetry, music, charades, masquerades, and improvised plays. Shakespeare had recently been adequately disclosed to German readers in the Schlegel-Tieck translation, and both Felix and Fanny reveled in the poet whom they could not yet read in the original. Their imaginative games and entertainments were inspired by this reading, and all their creative impulses, light or serious, were stimulated. Full of new ideas, they began to keep a common journal to which their comrades, old and young, added contributions. Every witty or amusing or poetical thing said or thought of was promptly recorded. At one time, we are told, they kept a supply of writing materials in the garden so that gushing of high spirits might not be checked by a trip back to the main house. They called this journal "The Garden Times," and added a sequel the following winter, "The Tea-and-Snow Times."

In this tide of happiness the *Midsummer Night's Dream* Overture was composed. We do not know to what extent his companions were aware of what occupied Felix's thoughts, and our guess now is far off and hardly to be trusted, but it is supposed that during the summer of 1826 he saw his father's park inhabited by Oberon, Titania and Puck, and fancied himself an actor in the lovely story, a very comprehensive actor, identifying himself with the human beings as well as with fairyland, with Bottom and his crew as well as with Theseus and Hermia and Helena.

Years afterwards he was to compose for *Midsummer Night's Dream* additional and equally famous music, but the Overture remains a perfect summary or translation of the play, a masterpiece in itself and a landmark in musical history. When he wrote it Mendelssohn was seventeen years old.

27

Music should be explained to the ear, not to the eye. It is hard to say on a printed page in what respects this Overture is a masterpiece. It is full of orchestral effects quite new, and of harmonic combinations which if not new in themselves, were employed in a new way. If we should study them on this page, the reader might be competent to hear the sounds in his imagination, or he might try them out on the piano, but neither process, certainly not the second, would give the orchestral color which is here the very essence. We marvel at the unerring instinct which led Mendelssohn to these novel effects. Apparently Shakespeare's poem-play had stimulated in him a musical dream, and by the untraceable operation of genius he had reached for the precise combination never before employed. The best way to study the Overture is to listen to an orchestral performance with a full score under your eyes. The next best way is to study a recording of an orchestral performance. Here also the score will be of great aid, even to those who are not yet skilful in reading the clefs.

At the beginning there is a succession of four soft chords, the first played by two flutes, the second by two flutes and two clarinets, the third by two flutes, two clarinets and two bassoons, the fourth by these instruments and two horns. In tone-color each chord differs from the preceding, and the whole sequence provokes an eerie mood. We hear the sequence again when the main theme is reintroduced halfway through the Overture, and again at the very end.

The quiet, slow effect of this passage is calculated to form a sharp contrast with the main theme, fast and scherzo-like, played staccato on the violins.

The second theme, also introduced by the violins, is song-like, a smooth, flowing pattern in contrast with the staccato effect.

Then follows, as in the characteristic first movements of sonatas and symphonies, a section in which both themes are developed and varied. The themes are then restated very much as at the beginning of the Overture. There is a short coda or "tail," and we hear at the close, played very softly, the chord sequence with which the piece began.

Some such analysis of the Overture might describe it as a composition, but for the effect of the music when it is played we need a different approach. What it says can be understood even by those who haven't read Shakespeare's play. The title, *Midsummer Night's Dream,* directs our interpretation of the music, but no strict program is laid down for the notes to illustrate; we are left free to imagine what we choose. Let me offer my interpretation, by way of challenge to you to make your own.

The four measures at the beginning always suggest to me moonlight and silence, the kind of silence that broods over a forest on a summer night, a promising silence—there may be at any moment the crackling of a twig or even the whir of wings.

When the main theme begins I see no fairy dance, no Puck-like spirits, but darting fireflies, pin points of light. The speed of the notes rouses and expresses intensity of feeling, much more than it suggests anything visual, and I delight in the changing colors of the tone, something that can be described only in a metaphor since it isn't color at all.

The second theme, as I said, has the quality of song, but just who is singing, I don't care to guess. Perhaps the singing is supposed to be done by me; at least the lyric theme, when it occurs, expresses my emotions. And when the sound fades away to the coda, to the pianissimo chord, I realize, since I have read Shakespeare's play, that Mendelssohn's music gives me very nearly the same kind of delight as Shakespeare's words.

We might pause here to consider this achievement, peculiar as I believe to Mendelssohn's genius. He can interpret Shakespeare or any other poet so long as he does not set the words to music. His gift is for saying the poetry over again *in* music rather than for enriching, by the addition of notes, words already beautiful. This opinion is not held by everybody, and you may find yourself protesting that Mendelssohn's songs have a charm of their own, and in some cases are still enormously popular, that he wrote oratorios and choral works, and that in the best of them he provided effective settings for the words. If your enthusiasm runs high, I should be sorry to bring it down. My point is simply that his talent for translating poetry into music was very rare, and he paid a natural penalty for it; he had the defect of this uncanny ability. When he has transferred the poetry to the music, we no longer need the text. It was not entirely by chance that he called his famous piano pieces "Songs Without Words." They are more song-like than his songs.

Mendelssohn wrote several operas, one of which, *Comacho's Wedding,* composed in 1825, was performed in 1827. It is the best of his attempts of this kind, and at its first performance received much applause. He knew it was imperfect, and when the second performance was postponed on account of the illness of a singer, he let the work die discreetly. He said that the libretto, based on an episode in *Don Quixote,* was not of sufficient importance. Several times later he expressed his desire for an adequate libretto, yet never found one. We may doubt whether any text would have proved satisfactory. The words would have been in his way.

Though we shall speak of his songs in another chapter, this is the right place to suggest, for a better understanding of the *Midsummer Night's Dream* Overture, that the reader compare Mendelssohn's songs with Schubert's, or the arias of his oratorios with those of Bach's and Handel's. The comparison makes clear how inseparable from the text is the music of Schubert, Bach, and Handel, and how easy it is, in recalling Mendelssohn's settings, to forget the words altogether. Schubert, Bach, and Handel, widely different in many respects, plant in us the conviction that they belong very much to this world, that they create out of human experience. Mendelssohn's best music seems to rise from experience ethereal rather than human, out of a world which haunts us but is not ours.

Mendelssohn gave us the kind of song which does not need words. In his weaker moments he was, as his detractors say, saccharine and sentimental. At his masterly best he evokes a beauty which startles the hearer, as though he had long been waiting for it and had given up hope, since to this day it is found so completely in no other composer.

CHAPTER FOUR

The Bach Revival

THE *Midsummer Night's Dream* OVER-ture had its first public performance in February, 1827, at Stettin, Mendelssohn conducting. It had already been played by an orchestra in the Garden House at Number 3 Leipzigerstrasse, and the composer had arranged it also as a piano duet. The speed with which this composition reached the public was far greater than so young a composer could reason-

33

ably hope for, but the family friends who had heard it intimately spread rumors of its excellence and prepared the way for it. So far Mendelssohn had been altogether fortunate. We should note here, however, that his meteoric success now began to produce inevitable antagonism among the critical or the envious. Opposition to him and his music began to show itself in Berlin, shortly developing to a point where a less healthy nature than his would have been discouraged, or perhaps embittered. He continued with outward equanimity his amazing activity in music and in the other occupations to which these early years were devoted, but from this time dates his dislike of Berlin, his feeling that so far as the arts were concerned it was an inhospitable city.

In May, 1826, he had matriculated at the University of Berlin. To qualify for entrance he submitted a verse translation of Terence's *Andria,* which would have attracted attention even if he had not been already a person of mark. It was the first German translation of Terence which preserved the original meters, and in this respect it set a fashion which scholarly renderings have usually followed. That a boy of seventeen could produce a work of classical scholarship so competent would astonish us now if we were not dealing with Mendelssohn. He had already produced a number of poems, some of them humorous, and the year he entered the University he wrote a short piece, four stanzas long, on the stupidity of critics. You will find it quoted on the last page of *Goethe and Mendelssohn*—quoted also with a transla-

34

tion in the article in *Grove's Dictionary*. At some time or other most artists have expressed the same reproachful sentiments but seldom with such vigor or conciseness.

So far as we know, he did not follow a complete University schedule, nor come up for a degree, but he heard Hegel lecture—on music, among other subjects, and he studied geography under Karl Ritter. His later facility in Italian suggests that he studied that language at the University, and from a sense of duty he gave some time to mathematics, though he disliked the subject and made no progress in it.

Along with academic courses he devoted himself at this time to certain sports in which he became highly proficient —riding, swimming, dancing, billiards. He was already well taught in drawing, and his landscape sketches, of which a large quantity remain, show talent and training considerably above amateur standards. His father's far-sighted generosity provided him also with constant travel. He knew his own country well, and already had an acquaintance with Europe beyond his years. All these studies and diversions, we should remember, were on the margin of his chief interest, which led him now to a remarkable contribution in the service of world culture.

The Berlin *Singakademie,* thanks to its founder, Karl Fasch, possessed a manuscript copy of Sebastian Bach's *St. Matthew Passion.* It seems not mere coincidence but manifest destiny that Zelter should have set value on this masterpiece, though he had never heard it performed, that Mendelssohn should have been his pupil, and strange to say, though himself a leader in the romantic age, should by his personal efforts have rescued the work from neglect and started the entirely modern and long-delayed cult of Bach. He here deserves full and somewhat exclusive credit. Fasch seems to have had no idea that any audience would find in Bach's larger works a supreme beauty as romantic as it is classical, a beauty which because it is supreme transcends all categories. Zelter, we know, was quite certain the Passion music would never be accepted without much editing, and even then the appreciative audience would be small. Had the decision been left entirely to him, the greatest of oratorios would not have been performed.

When Mendelssohn first studied the manuscript at the *Singakademie,* his admiration of the music soon became known to his family. He spoke of it repeatedly. To please him, his grandmother had the manuscript copied for a Christmas gift in 1823. Mendelssohn studied the score until he literally knew it by heart. It is said that at the rehearsals, when it was at last performed, he would call out the corrections without consulting the page. No sooner had he mastered the work than he began to try out different passages whenever a group of singers met at his father's house. In 1827 this casual study of the *St. Matthew Passion* developed into a serious project. He organized a chorus of sixteen voices to rehearse every Saturday evening. Eduard Devrient, the baritone, was in the group, soon to become as enthusiastic a devotee of Bach as Mendelssohn himself.

It may have been Devrient who suggested that the Passion should be given in public by the *Singakademie,* which numbered three or four hundred voices, and that Mendelssohn should conduct the rehearsals and the performance. Felix was only twenty years old, and he had no illusions about the probable reception of such a proposal. Berlin was proud of Zelter and of his singers; what would be thought of a very young man who offered to take over the baton and demonstrate the importance of music which Zelter preferred not to perform? Mendelssohn's parents commended his reluctance to challenge public opinion, but others, and particularly Devrient, thought it unforgivable to let the opportunity pass. He persuaded Felix to go with him and lay the proposal before Zelter.

We wish we had a verbatim report of the interview. Zelter at first was stunned, perhaps more than a little annoyed, but after a brisk exchange of argument he took the generous course and handed over the *Singakademie* to his pupil. From January, 1829, until the performance on March 11, the rehearsals proceeded, and the city filled with gossip about the bold experiment. The soloists were recruited from the Opera. From each rehearsal chorus and orchestra came away in greater excitement. When the momentous hour arrived, the house was sold out and more than a thousand ticket-seekers were turned away.

No doubt the performance was magnificent, but it would be impossible now to estimate it on purely musical grounds. Since Bach performed the work with his own choir in his own church, it had lain silent and forgotten.

37

The effect of its resurrection must have been overwhelming. For the first time the greatest of German composers received adequate recognition, at the hands of a youth whose love of music had in it no impulse of selfishness or self-advancement.

The circumstances surrounding the performance of the Passion by the *Singakademie* are known to us through certain passages in Fanny's letters to Karl Klingemann, a dear friend of the family, the librettist of *Comacho's Wedding,* who had gone recently to England as Secretary to the Hannover Legation. By piecing together all the references to her brother's work we see that he had for some time been co-operating closely with Zelter in the *Akademie's* programs. On December 8, 1828, Fanny writes that Felix has composed an elaborate piece for four choruses on the Latin text beginning, "Hora est, jam nos de somno surgere." (Now it is high time to awake from sleep.) The *Akademie,* she adds, will sing it. On December 27 she writes that Felix is arranging Handel's Cantata, *Acis and Galatea* for an *Akademie* performance, and in return "the *Akademie* will sing the Passion for him and Devrient. It is to be sung in the course of the winter for some charitable purpose." In the spring, she adds, Felix will leave for a journey to England.

From these brief references it is evident that there was some bartering before the *Akademie* authorities gave their permission to revive Bach's work, not the least of the stipulation being that the performance would be outside the usual schedule, an extra concert for charity. Even had we no other evidence we should understand that others besides Zelter had to be won over, and their confidence was at no time completely gained. On March 22, 1829, Fanny gives a full account of both concerts. We quote this important letter, using with some changes Karl Klingemann's translation.

"We send you Felix before long. He will be remembered here for the two crowded performances of the Passion for the benefit of the poor. What used to be a dream, to be realized perhaps in the distant future, has now come true; the Passion has been heard in public, and now belongs to the world. . . . Felix and Devrient had talked for a long time of a possible performance, but the plan had no definite form until one evening at our house they made up their minds, and walked off the next morning in brand new yellow kid gloves (they thought these important) to the managers of the *Akademie*. They were very diplomatic in their approach and at first merely asked whether they might be allowed the use of the concert hall for a charitable purpose. As the music they would perform was likely to be successful, they offered to give a second concert for the benefit of the *Akademie*. This the managers declined with thanks, insisting instead on a fixed payment of fifty *thalers,* all profit to go to the concert-givers. Incidentally that reply of theirs now bothers them. Zelter made no objection, and the rehearsals began on the Friday following. Felix went over the whole score, made a few judicious cuts, and only instrumented the recitative, 'And the veil of the temple was rent in twain.' Everything else was left untouched. The people were astonished, stared, admired; and when, after a few weeks, the rehearsals in the *Akademie* itself commenced, their faces became *very* long with surprise at the existence of such a work, about which they, the members of the Berlin *Akademie,* knew nothing. After having got over their astonishment, they began to study with true, warm interest. The thing itself, the novelty and originality of the form, took hold of them, the subject was universally comprehensible and engaging, and Devrient sang the recitatives most beautifully. The happiness and enthusiasm shown by all the singers during the very first rehearsals, and which each new rehearsal kindled to increasing love and ardor; the delight and surprise created by each new element—the solos, the orchestra, Felix's splendid interpretation and his accompanying the first rehearsals at the piano from beginning to end *by heart,* all these were moments never to be forgotten. Zelter, who helped at the first rehearsals, gradually retreated, and during the later rehearsals, as well as at the concerts, with praiseworthy resignation took his seat among the audience. And now the members of the *Akademie* themselves spread such a favorable report about the music, and such a general and vivid interest was created in all classes, that on the very day after the first advertisement of the concert all the tickets were taken, and during the latter days upwards of a thousand people applied in vain. On Wednesday, March 10, the first performance took place, and excepting a few slight mistakes of the solo-singers it

40

may be called a perfect success. . . . As soon as the doors were opened the people, who already had been long waiting outside, rushed into the hall, which was quite full in less than a quarter of an hour. I sat at the corner, where I could see Felix very well, and had gathered the strongest alto-voices around me. The choruses were sung with a fire, a striking power, and also with a touching delicacy and softness the like of which I have never heard, except at the second concert, when they surpassed themselves. Taking for granted that you still remember its dramatic form, I send you the text, just mentioning that the account of the evangelist was sung by Stümer, the words of Jesus by Devrient, of Peter by Bader, the High-priest and Pilate by Busolt, Judas by Weppler. Mmes. Schätzel, Milder, and Türrschmiedt sang the soprano and alto parts exquisitely. The room was crowded, and had all the air of a church, the deepest quiet and most solemn devotion everywhere, only now and then involuntary utterances of intense emotion. What is so often erroneously maintained of like undertakings was true of this, that a peculiar spirit pervaded the concert, so that everybody did his best, and many did more. Rietz, for instance, who with the help of his brother and brother-in-law had undertaken to copy the parts of all the different instruments, refused all pay for himself and the other two. Most singers declined accepting the tickets offered to them, or else paid for them. . . ."

If Mendelssohn, as we believe, threw himself into this important enterprise from no selfish or self-seeking motive, it is clear from Fanny's letters and from other sources that a minority in Berlin held a different opinion. After the first performance of the Passion an attempt was made to prevent the second, even though there was a wide demand for it. Felix and Devrient overcame this ill-timed opposition by a course not likely to win over his critics; he went directly to the Crown Prince, who ordered the performance to proceed.

For the first concert six free tickets had been given. For the second, none at all. To accommodate an increased audience, all available rooms adjacent to the main hall were thrown open. The great music was rendered even more beautifully than before, the improvement showing especially in the chorus and the orchestra. Except for an unfortunate mistake on the part of one of the soloists, Fanny considered the performance perfect, and the city at large agreed, but Felix had reason to know that the unclouded good fortune of his youth was now, because of his very success, coming to an end. Henceforth he might expect the usual fate of a great artist, the persistent hostility of some of those less great.

It has been said that the musicians of Berlin resented his youth, the wealth to which he had been born, the influence which his friends exerted on his behalf. All this would be natural enough. In fairness we must add, however, that something in his manner at this time gave offense. He may have been a little peremptory, somewhat too sure of himself, or he may have allowed his Berlin colleagues to feel his own hostility to the North German temperament. His letters at this time and later contain complaints of Berlin manners, of the frigid solemnity, the ominous silence with which even cultivated people listened to music in a home, the noncommittal gloom which they thought it was their duty to put on when brought face to face with art. The Royal Orchestra, by his own report, were so prejudiced that they refused to be led by him in public. He says justly that perhaps he had no right to feel hurt, being still at the beginning of his career, but he was glad to go abroad for a while, to a foreign country, before inviting again the judgment of his own people.

CHAPTER FIVE

England

MENDELSSOHN BEGAN HIS FIRST JOUR-
ney to England on April 10, 1829. His
father and his younger sister Rebecca
went with him as far as Hamburg, where
on the 18th he took the steamer *Attwood*
for London, arriving on Tuesday, the
21st. Steamboats were then a recent and
not yet dependable invention. The *Attwood* met bad weather and its engine
broke down, all the passengers were sea-

sick, and for two days of the voyage Mendelssohn says he had one fainting fit after the other. He was disgusted with himself and everything about the boat, he cursed England for having been very indirectly the cause of his misery, and he damned particularly the concert overture which he had recently finished, "A Calm Sea and a Prosperous Voyage." But the night before he landed, the weather cleared, there was a beautiful moon and hundreds of vessels around them most companionably, and the next morning he had the thrill of the passage up the Thames through green meadows and little towns with smoke-belching chimneys, and at last the tremendous sight of London.

From that moment as long as he lived he was a fanatical lover of England. No other part of the world so well suited his temperament, no other people understood him so completely or rated him and his music so high. We shall not give an account of all his visits to Great Britain nor of even this first visit in full detail; to do so would greatly extend the length of this book. But we should glance at the various explanations of his fondness for England and of England's devotion to him.

When he arrived in London that April noon, the so-called Victorian age was still eight years away, but the important liberating and constructive movements which later became associated with Victoria's reign were already starting — Parliamentary reform, religious toleration, social betterment among workers in the towns, improvement of conditions among the farming class by the gradual lowering and final abolition of tariffs. To us now the degree of progress, except in the matter of tariffs, seems a bit modest, but for the time England was well ahead of most European countries, and was conscious of the fact. The wars at the end of the eighteenth century and the Napoleonic wars had bankrupted her and reduced the working classes to keen misery, but by 1829 she had so far recovered that a new age, perhaps the most splendid period in her history, was well in sight. Mendelssohn's ship brought him to a land of confidence, of expanding hope, of enlarged curiosity. Nowhere else in Europe could he have found a public frame of mind more completely in accord with his own.

In many respects the British musical taste was predisposed towards him. Choral music, especially male choirs, are what might be called an English specialty. Songs or ballads, choral works and church music, have largely occupied the talents of the British composer. Most of all, perhaps, church music. The well-established choirs in the numerous cathedrals, school and college chapels, and parish churches, provided attractive careers, social prestige, and financial security such as the composer, the singer, and the organist could look for in no other country except Germany, and even in Germany a musician who limited his activities to the church rarely received the social or other rewards of his English colleague. To a country which liked and which could appreciate church music and organ playing, the steamship *Attwood* brought a youth who by the general testimony of English organists

46

themselves was the best player they had heard, and a composer of choral works who had recently revived the *St. Matthew Passion,* and whose study of Bach established a certain kinship with their own great musicians of the seventeenth and eighteenth centuries.

The immediate acceptance by the English of Mendelssohn and his music was for him an unexpected and heartening contrast with the professional jealousies he had encountered in Berlin. Had he been older this critical antagonism might not have weighed so heavily upon him, nor perhaps would the English applause have so startled and inspired him. But his destiny once more was kind; the music lovers of an entire nation became his friends at the very moment when he needed their friendship.

Whether he did as much for England as England did for him, we now have some doubts. Like Handel at an earlier time, he sidetracked by his enormous popularity the beautiful and characteristic tradition of the old English masters. Throughout the Victorian age English churches and English homes fairly reeked with sweetish imitations of Mendelssohn, not always of him at his best. It is only since the beginning of the present century that British composers have again emerged as an important, even formidable, school. In the winter of 1896-97 I heard the American composer, Edward Alexander MacDowell, say how important to English music, indeed to world music, the work of Henry Purcell had been, and no doubt again would be. With the courage of extreme youth I confessed my complete ignorance of Purcell. "For that," he replied, "blame yourself partly, but much more Georg Friedrich Handel and Felix Mendelssohn. They submerged Purcell, but sooner or later he will come up to breathe."

Of course no artist can be blamed for achieving and exerting an enormous influence. If the English people and Mendelssohn, as has frequently been said, fell in love at sight and never let their affections cool, it's perhaps a little ungracious and certainly unfair to blame Mendelssohn for having been too fascinating. We pause in the story merely to note that the long and sustained admiration of Mendelssohn has now its reaction, and English intellectuals sometimes dispose of him with benevolent condescension, as though he had been an immature experience now outgrown. Purcell and the other long neglected composers have indeed come up to breathe, and in the nationalism of the moment Mendelssohn suffers. The pendulum will some day swing again.

The first English visit is reported fully in Mendelssohn's letters to his family. Klingemann and Moscheles were waiting for him on the dock and took him to lodgings at a house in Great Portland Street, numbered then 103, later 79, at the corner of Ridinghouse Street. These quarters may have been chosen because the landlord, Heinke, was a German. Though Mendelssohn's English improved quickly, the language bothered him a little at first.

In his letter of April 25 he gives his first crowded impressions. "It is fearful! It is maddening! I am quite giddy and confused. London is the grandest and most complicated monster on the face of the earth. How can I compress into one letter what I have been three days seeing? I hardly remember the chief events, and yet I must not keep a diary, for then I should see less of life, and that must not be. On the contrary, I want to catch hold of whatever offers itself. Things roll and whirl around me and carry me along as in a vortex. Not in the last six months at Berlin have I seen so many contrasts and such variety as in these three days. Could you but once, turning to the right from my lodging, walk down Regent Street and see the wide bright street with its arcades (alas! it is enveloped in a thick fog today!) and the shops with letters as big as men, and the stage-coaches piled up with people, and a row of vehicles outrun by the foot-passengers because in one place the smart carriages have stopped the way! Here a horse prances to a house where its rider has friends. There you see men used as ambulating advertisement-boards on which the most graceful achievements of accomplished cats are promised. Then there are beggars, negroes, and those fat John Bulls with their slender, beautiful two daughters hanging on their arms. Ah, those daughters! However, do not be alarmed, there's no danger in that quarter, neither in Hyde Park, so rich in ladies, where I drove about yesterday in a fashionable way with Mme. Moscheles, nor in the concerts, nor in the opera (I have been to all these places already) ; only at the corners and crossings there *is* danger, and there I sometimes say to myself softly, in a well-known voice, 'Take care lest you get run over.' Such a whirl, such a roar! But I will become historical, and quietly relate my doings, else you will learn nothing about me."

The day he arrived in London Mendelssohn was taken by Klingemann to an English coffee house, and there reading in the *Times* that *Otello* would be given that night, Malibran in the role of Desdemona, he resolved to go, though not yet recovered from seasickness. For his seat in the pit of the King's Theatre he paid half a guinea and found himself in a large house decorated chiefly in red, with six tiers of boxes, crimson-curtained, out of which gazed the fashionable ladies, decked in great white feathers, gold chains, jewels. The strong scent of pomade and perfume, he says, gave him a headache, which explains perhaps his severe criticism of Malibran, who impressed him as beautiful and immensely gifted both as singer and actress, but so disposed to exaggerate that her passionate scenes became mere screaming and raving. He left the performance at a quarter to one, when Desdemona was finally smothered. The endurance of the British audience astonished him. After the opera a ballet, *La sonambule,* was scheduled, and in his letter he wonders when the audience reached home.

His first weeks were devoted to sight-seeing, to making new acquaintances, and to much music in private gatherings. He speaks of his enjoyment of the grand piano which the Clementis sent to his room, and of the cheerful coal fire which made that apartment attractive. What he says of London shows that he traveled with the eye of

a painter. "I think the town and the streets quite beautiful. Again I was struck with awe when yesterday I drove
in an open carriage to the City, along a different road,
and everywhere found the same flow of life, everywhere
green, red, yellow bills stuck on the houses from top to
bottom, or gigantic letters painted on them, everywhere
noise and smoke, everywhere the end of the streets lost in
fog. Every few moments I passed a church, or a market-
place, or a green square, or a theatre, or caught a glimpse
of the Thames, on which the steamers can now go right
through the town under all the bridges, because an invention has been made for letting down the large funnels,
in the way masts are lowered. Last but not least, to see
the masts from the West India Docks stretching their
heads over the housetops, and to see a harbor as big as
the Hamburg one treated like a mere pond, with sluices,
and the ships arranged not singly but in rows, like regi-
ments—to see all that makes one's heart rejoice at the
greatness of the world."

His first professional appearance in London was with
the Philharmonic on May 25, where he conducted his
Symphony in C minor. His letter of the following day
describes the success of both the rehearsal and the performance. The Philharmonic concerts were then held in
the Argyll Rooms in Regent Street, and when he arrived
for the rehearsal he found not only the orchestra but an
audience of at least two hundred, chiefly ladies. His social
success was evidently in full tide. When the moment
came for his Symphony, he got up on the stage and took

out his white baton, made especially for the occasion. The concertmeister introduced him to the orchestra, and there was much bowing and smiling, and after the Symphony had been played, orchestra and audience applauded vigorously, the violinists, he says, showing their approval by knocking their instruments with their bows and stamping their feet. At the end of the rehearsal all the players and most of the by-standers wished to shake hands, an exercise which Mendelssohn found highly flattering but when practiced in quantity fatiguing.

The concert was a brilliant triumph. Instead of the Minuet and Trio of the Symphony, he played the lovely Scherzo from the Octet, which was so vigorously encored that he felt obliged to repeat it. Later when the Symphony was published he dedicated it to the Philharmonic, and they elected him an honorary member of the Society.

Other concerts followed quickly. On the afternoon of May 30 he played with the Orchestra Weber's "Concertstück," and in order to try the piano he arrived at the Argyll Rooms in advance of the hour and began practicing. So completely did he lose himself that he didn't notice the audience silently slipping in to enjoy the unexpected entertainment. The *Times* of the following day records its astonished admiration that he played the Concerto with no music before him.

At another concert the *Midsummer Night's Dream* Overture was performed, and he played the E flat Concerto of Beethoven. On June 13, at a charity concert for the relief of victims of the floods in Silesia, the *Mid-*

summer Night's Dream Overture was repeated, and with Moscheles he played his own Concerto in E for two pianos. A few days later, somewhat to his amusement, an invitation arrived from Sir Alexander Johnston, Governor of Ceylon, to compose a festival song for the natives, who wished to celebrate their emancipation.

The picture galleries of London impressed him deeply, and his letters are full of praise for their treasures, but the English theatre disappointed him on the whole. His description of Kemble in *Hamlet* recalls to us with a shock the condition of the stage at that time. The criticism may serve to imply that the German theatre was further advanced, but perhaps Mendelssohn was judging the London performance by his own instinctive good taste, which was far ahead of his time.

"In the evening I went with Rosen, Mühlenfels, and Klingemann to Covent Garden: 'Hamlet.' I believe, children, that he was right who said that the English sometimes do not understand Shakespeare. At least this representation was extravagant; and yet Kemble played Hamlet, and in his way played him well. But, alas! that way is crazy, and ruins the whole piece. His appearing, for instance, with one yellow and one black leg, to indicate madness, his falling before the ghost in order to strike an attitude, his screaming out the end of every little phrase in that regular applause-exacting high tone of his, his behaving altogether like a John Bull Oxford student, and not like a Danish crown prince, all that might pass. But that he should not the least enter into poor Shakespeare's intention as to killing the king, and therefore coolly skip that scene where the king prays and Hamlet comes in and goes out again without having made up his mind for the deed (to my taste one of the finest passages of the piece), and that he constantly behaves like a *bravado,* treating the king in such a way that he deserves to be shot down at once, for instance during the play on the stage threatening him with his fist and shouting into his ear the words that he should have quietly dropped— these are things not to be pardoned. Of course Laertes and Hamlet do not jump into Ophelia's tomb and wrestle there, for they never guess why they should do so; and at the end, when Hamlet falls down and says, 'The rest is silence,' and I expected a flourish and Fortinbras, Horatio actually leaves the prince, hastily comes forward to the lamps, and says, 'Ladies and gentlemen, tomorrow evening "The Devil's Elixir." ' Thus ended 'Hamlet' in England. Of what they skip or abridge one might make a tragedy in itself; the instructions of Polonius; the leave-taking of Laertes from Ophelia, half of a monologue of Hamlet, etc., never appear. Some things, however, they gave excellently, for instance the grave-digger scene. The old clown made wonderfully coarse jests, and sang his song in the grave unmusically and very, very beautifully. Ophelia too in her madness once sang quite madly; whilst the others were talking she murmured a low melody; the fencing and changing of rapiers, too, was done very cleverly. But what is all that? There is little poetry in England. Really!"

In July he left with Klingemann for a tour in Scotland. After brief pauses at York and Durham, they arrived in Edinburgh and found lodgings in Princes Street. What the picturesque city must have said to his many-sided genius! The effect of this journey on his later composing is well known. From Scottish landscape and Scottish history he laid up a rich source of inspiration. At twilight one day he and Klingemann visited Holyrood, saw the little room with the winding staircase leading up to the door, recalled that up these stairs came the assassins and found Rizzio, and in a dark corner near by murdered him. "The chapel close to it is now roofless. Grass and ivy grow there, and at that broken altar Mary was crowned Queen of Scotland. Everything around is broken and mouldering, and the bright sky shines in. I believe I found today in that old chapel the beginning of my Scotch Symphony."

On July 31st Klingemann sent the Berlin household a brilliant account of their visit to Abbottsford and their memorable hours with Sir Walter Scott. The great man, he says, understood their importance and treated them royally. Mendelssohn had to write music in Scott's album, and Klingemann improvised some verses, which he quotes in full. In a postscript, however, Felix sets the family right. There wasn't a word of truth in the letter; Klingemann was simply making the report which a tourist would like to make. They had found Sir Walter in the act of leaving Abbottsford, they had stared at him like idiots, unable at first to think of a thing to say, and when at last they got started their superficial conversation had lasted for no more than half an hour.

After Edinburgh they visited the Highlands. Klingemann continued to write the larger part of the letters, though sticking closer to the facts, Felix adding a postscript, until he arrived in Wales, where he records with humorous details the deplorable state of the popular music as evidenced by the unfortunate duets of harpers and hurdy-gurdies in the roadside inns.

Back in London he prepared for an early return. His sister Fanny was to marry Wilhelm Hensel on October 3. But on September 10 a carriage in which Mendelssohn was riding was upset, and he received an injury to his knee which kept him in bed for nearly two months. The kindness of all his English friends during this period of inconvenience and suffering meant more to him than his triumphs.

On his way home at last he wrote at Calais on November 29: "So England lies behind me and my visit is past and gone. It is a beautiful and beloved land, and when its white coast disappeared and the black French coast came in view, I felt as though I had taken leave of a friend, and as if all the dear kind people were once more nodding to me."

CHAPTER SIX

Rome and Paris

MENDELSSOHN'S FIRST VISIT TO ENG-
land had been planned as part of a
larger tour, and he returned to Berlin
only for a brief pause with his family
before setting out on the second stage of
his wanderings, as far south as Naples
and north again to Paris. He hoped to be
accompanied by other members of the
household, at least by his parents, but his
mother's poor health interfered with this

57

plan, and his own departure was delayed until late spring by an attack of the measles. But the winter in Number 3 Leipzigerstrasse was unusually happy for several reasons; he was glad to be at home, he was glad to find Fanny and her husband living in the Garden House, so close at hand that their old companionship was unbroken, and it gave him pleasure to be offered the chair of music, founded especially for him at the University of Berlin. He declined the invitation, wishing to continue his composing and fearing to exchange a practical career for an academic one. But the evidence of approval and good will on the part of governmental authorities balanced to some extent at least the local jealousies of his professional colleagues. During this winter he composed his Symphony in D ("Reformation" Symphony) for the anniversary of the Augsburg Confession, celebrated June 25, 1830, and many shorter pieces, among them, we believe, first sketches of some of the "Songs Without Words."

On May 13 the deferred travels were resumed, his father accompanying him a short distance. On the 20th he reached Weimar and spent a fortnight in that last visit to Goethe already described. On June 6 he reached Munich, where he stayed for a month.

We lack space here to give a complete account of his way of living while on tour. Years afterwards his brother Paul edited a volume of travel letters covering these years from 1830 to 1832. They should be studied closely. The record of each day shows how completely Mendelssohn carried along with him his well-disciplined habits of work, indeed his total life, except for the absence of his family. Wherever he stopped for more than the briefest stay he installed a piano in his room and spent the mornings practicing or composing. The afternoons he liked to spend out of doors with his sketchbook, his paints, or his crayons. In the late afternoons and evenings he enjoyed the society, wherever he happened to be, of the best musicians and writers, of all who were notable in any way. We wonder at the organization of his waking hours which enabled him to accomplish so much and yet to see so many people. He was still a very young man, and he was traveling alone; nothing but his good sense and strength of character made possible such good use of time.

Helpful as his travels were to the development of his art, he perhaps was doing himself another service not planned in advance. The charm of his personality, which we now can only imagine from the innumerable reports of it, was felt in every city he visited, and thanks to the extent of his journeys he became a well known personality throughout a large part of Europe. Not every genius has been loved for himself as much as for his works, and in some cases the works get a friendlier reception if the genius keeps in the background, but Mendelssohn himself had attracted attention everywhere, quite apart from his music.

His travel letters reveal clearly the breadth and intelligence of his interests, his attention to the life of the people in each town, his eye for beautiful landscape, his discriminating enjoyment of works of art, and his constant meditation on musical problems. Not a little of the philosophizing tendency which had distinguished his grandfather was reborn in him. At the end of the long tour he wrote home that he had made, he was certain, good use of his opportunities, gathering impressions and clarifying his own purposes in life. We smile a little at so modest a statement. The acquaintance with new places excited him to extraordinary sensitiveness, and the long letters record minute details of conversation, fragments of the music he heard, even of chance singing in the streets, colors in the landscape, peculiarities of the various church organs he played on, even the pitch of the bells in town clocks sounding the hour. And his attention, we should remember again, had not been on music alone. His eye was busy. More than once his descriptions of landscape are supplemented by excellent drawings.

If the journey helped him to expand in new directions, it taught him also to define his genius sharply. His first visit to Paris while he was yet a boy had given him little pleasure, but he had ascribed the disappointment then to the French lack of appreciation for the German composers whom he himself loved. On this Italian tour he now realized that with all his admiration for Italy he would never care much for Italian music. He was a German. In his opinion the Latin genius had passed its prime. Whatever else he might still learn from it he could never admire its spirit. "The days when every Italian was a born musician," he writes in one place, "if indeed they ever existed, are long gone by." He tries to find a reason for his dislike of Latin culture in his admiration for the Italian landscape, asking why Italy should insist on being the land of art when it is really the land of nature. A letter from Rome dated January 17, 1831, puts his point of view most clearly.

"We in Germany may perhaps wish to accomplish something false or impossible, but it is, and always will be, quite *dissimilar;* and just as a *cicisbeo* will forever be odious and repulsive to my feelings, so is it also with Italian music. I may be too obtuse to comprehend either: but I shall never feel otherwise; and recently, at the Philharmonic, after the music of Pacini and Bellini, when the Cavaliere Ricci begged me to accompany him in 'Non più andrai,' the very first notes were so utterly different and so infinitely remote from all the previous music, that the matter was clear to me then, and never will it be equalized, so long as there is such a blue sky, and such a charming winter as the present. In the same way the Swiss can paint no beautiful scenery, precisely because they have it the whole day before their eyes. 'Les Allemands traitent la musique comme une affaire d'état,' said Spontini, and I accept the omen. I lately heard some musicians here talking of their composers, and I listened in silence. One quoted ———, but the others interrupted him, saying he could not be considered an Italian, for the German school still clung to him, and he had never been able to get rid of it; consequently he had never been at home in Italy; we Germans say precisely the reverse of him, and it must be not a little trying to find yourself so *entre deux,* and without any fatherland. So far as I am concerned I stick to my own colors, which are quite honorable enough for me."

Mendelssohn's comments on the musical conditions he found at Munich, the first important stop on his journey, are as critical as anything he wrote of Italy, and it seems that they contradict his own statement that he stood for the German rather than the Italian taste, yet he understood himself correctly. His dislike of the Latin temperament and his failure to understand it could never be completely cured, whereas his remarks about Munich had to do with a temporary condition. He may even have felt, by way of excuse, that Bavaria was under a bad Italian influence. The Munich passage occurs in a letter describing a performance of *Fidelio.*

"Schechner is very much gone off; the quality of her voice has become husky; she repeatedly sang flat, yet there were moments when her expression was so touching, that I wept in my own fashion; all the others were bad, and there was also much to censure in the performance. Still, there is great talent in the orchestra; and the style in which they played the overture was very good. Certainly our Germany is a strange land; producing great people, but not appreciating them; possessing many fine singers and intellectual artists, but none sufficiently modest and subordinate to render their parts faithfully, and without false pretension. Marzelline introduces all sorts of flourishes into her part; Jaquino is a blockhead; the minister a simpleton: and when a German like Beethoven writes an opera, then comes a German like Stuntz or Poissl (or whoever it may have been) and strikes out the *ritournelle,* and similar unnecessary passages; another German adds a trombone part to his symphonies; a third declares that Beethoven is overloaded: and thus is a great man sacrificed."

From Munich Mendelssohn went to Vienna, which he reached on August 13. On October 9 he was in Venice, on October 22 in Florence. On November 1 he reached Rome, where he spent the winter, until April 10, 1831, living at Number 5 Piazza di Spagna. From then until the end of May he was at Naples, then back to Rome for two weeks, then by leisurely stages to Genoa, Milan, the Italian Lakes, Geneva, Lucerne, and Munich, which he reached in the early autumn.

The long stay in Rome was naturally the most interesting part of the tour. The antiquities of the city fascinated him, the famous churches, especially St. Peter's, the treasures of painting and sculpture, the surrounding landscape. In Rome he finished the "Hebrides" Overture and worked on the *Walpurgis Nacht* and both the "Italian" and "Scotch" Symphonies. But with all his sightseeing and composing he found time to spend with new friends, most of them famous artists. Bertel Thorwaldsen, the Danish sculptor, appealed to him particularly. On December 20, 1830, he writes:

"My piano playing is a source of gratification to me here. Thorwaldsen loves music, and I sometimes play to him in the morning while he is at work. He has an excel-

lent instrument in his studio, and when I look at the old
gentleman and see him kneading his brown clay, or per-
fecting an arm or a folded drapery, when I see him
creating what will be admired as an enduring work, I am
happy that I can give him any pleasure. . . . The 'Hebrides'
is completed at last, and strange production it is. . . . After
the New Year I intend to write several things for the
piano, and probably some kind of symphony. Two have
been running through my head."

On February 22, 1831, he gives us an account of the
Walpurgis Nacht and of the "Scotch" Symphony:

"Since I left Vienna I have partly composed Goethe's
first Walpurgis Nacht, but have not yet had courage to
write it down. The composition has now assumed form
and become a grand Cantata, with full orchestra, and may
turn out well. At the opening there are songs of spring,
etc., and plenty of others of the same kind. Afterwards,
when the watchmen with their 'Gabeln, und Zacken, und
Eulen,' make a great noise, the fairy frolics begin, and
you know that I have a particular foible for them; the
sacrificial Druids then appear, with their trombones in
C major, when the watchmen come in again in alarm, and
here I mean to introduce a light mysterious tripping
chorus; and lastly to conclude with a grand sacrificial
hymn. Don't you think this might develop into a new
style of Cantata? I have an instrumental introduction, as
a matter of course, and the effect of the whole is very
spirited. I hope it will soon be finished. I have once more
begun to compose with fresh vigor, and the 'Italian'

symphony makes rapid progress; it will be the most sportive piece I have yet composed, especially the last movement. I have not yet decided on the *adagio,* and think I shall reserve it for Naples. . . . The 'Scotch' symphony alone is not yet quite to my liking; if any brilliant idea occurs to me, I will seize it at once, quickly write it down, and finish it at last."

Later he wrote his friend Devrient that the *Walpurgis Nacht* was finished. He began it, he says, simply to please himself, but now it is done he thinks it may be a successful concert piece, since he has found that what he composes with least thought of the public, the public are most certain to like.

On his second visit to Munich he received a commission to compose an opera for the Munich Theatre. We don't think of him now as an operatic composer, in spite of his youthful attempts in that form. We forget that till the end of his life he was looking for the ideal libretto, quite convinced that opera was his field if only a suitable text could be found. All that he wrote on the subject, however, convinces us that in this one point he entirely misunderstood his gifts. There were strong dramatic elements in his music, but for the actual theatre he probably had little talent. Shakespeare and Goethe were for him poets to read and to translate, not into action but into beautiful tones. He dreamt, like so many literary men, of a theatre as lofty and unearthly as our imaginings of Hamlet or Macbeth while we are meeting them in the book. The wear and tear of the actual theatre, the inevitable adjustments and compromises and reconciliations, would have been for him impossible, but he never recognized that fact; he believed in opera as an art form, and looked forward to the happy moment when a sympathetic collaborator should present himself.

In December he arrived in Paris for his second and last visit to that city. This time he found there much more to enjoy, though he always remained critical of the French attitude toward music. The *Societé des Concerts* gave a performance of the *Midsummer Night's Dream* Overture on February 19, 1832, and at another concert on March 18 he played with the same orchestra Beethoven's Concerto in G. For a short time his music had something of a vogue in Paris, perhaps because he himself, with his usual ease, won instant and wide popularity.

Through his friend Ferdinand Hiller he met Chopin, Meyerbeer, Liszt, and Ole Bull, and indulged himself, as he says, in a whirl of social engagements. He spent much time with Chopin, whose frail health and languid manner contrasted strangely with his own inexhaustible energy. For the Polish composer he felt at once deep respect, and to a certain degree, appreciation. Perhaps he admired his piano technique more than his compositions. He admitted frankly that Chopin's fingers could get effects impossible for him, but he objected to the constant use of rubato, and in the compositions he failed to understand a kind of poetry totally different from the cheerful fantasy of, let us say, the *Midsummer Night's Dream* scherzo. Ferdinand Hiller, who had occasion at this time to see the two often

together, says that Mendelssohn played best the music of
Bach, Mozart, Beethoven, or himself. The music of other
composers did not come off so well at his hands, certainly
not the music of Chopin. The obvious truth is that though
both men were generous in recognizing any kind of talent,
the temperamental gulf between them was very wide.

With Liszt, Mendelssohn had more in common. Liszt
and he were musicians in the large sense, composers not
only for the piano but for all instruments and for choral
groups. They both, each in his own way, were drawn toward church music. They both had the histrionic equipment of the natural performer and liked to conquer a
large audience, yet they both respected, though they might
not understand, Chopin's sensitive reticence, his amazing
originality, and within the field to which he limited himself, the perfection of his art.

Much of his time in Paris Mendelssohn spent in the
theatre, and his letters home show that the Munich opera
commission was constantly on his mind. His father advised him to look for a good play among the French
dramatists, have it translated, and turn it into a libretto.
Mendelssohn's reply in his letter of December 19, 1831,
has been quoted so often that it is almost famous. Before
he left Germany, he reminds his father, he had asked Karl
Immermann, of Düsseldorf, to furnish a libretto, and of
course he could make no other arrangement now until he
saw what Immermann would write. The elder Mendelssohn had been disgusted by the arrangement. Karl Immermann was a very minor poet indeed, known chiefly in

Düsseldorf, no doubt an admirable character but unacquainted with the requirements of the stage or with public taste.

In the well known letter Mendelssohn replies to these objections, and makes clear, unconsciously, the causes in himself which would prevent him from ever composing an opera.

"I believed," he said, "that I was acting quite to your satisfaction when I made Immermann my offer. Besides, some new poems that he read to me convinced me more than ever that he was a true poet, and where I had a choice of equal merit, I would always decide in favor of a German rather than a French libretto. Furthermore, he has fixed on a subject which has been long in my thoughts, and which, if I am not mistaken, my mother wished to see made into an opera—I mean, Shakespeare's 'Tempest.' ... From what I know of Immermann I feel assured of a first rate libretto. . . .

"None of the new libretti here would in my opinion have any success whatever, if brought out for the first time on a German stage. One of the distinctive characteristics of them all, is precisely of a nature that I should resolutely oppose, although the taste of the present day may demand it, and I quite admit that it is wiser to go with the current than to struggle against it. I allude to immorality. In 'Robert le Diable' the nuns come one after the other to allure the hero of the piece, till at last the abbess succeeds in doing so: the same hero is conveyed by magic into the apartment of her whom he loves, and casts her from him in an attitude which the public here applauds, and probably all Germany will do the same; she then implores his mercy in a grand aria. In another opera a young girl divests herself of her garments, and sings a song to the effect that next day at this time she will be married; all this is effective, but I have no music for such things. I consider it ignoble, so if the present epoch exacts this style and considers it indispensable, then I will write oratorios."

CHAPTER SEVEN

Songs Without Words

MENDELSSOHN'S DISCONTENT WITH
Paris was increased by a series of mis-
fortunes which occurred during the last
weeks of his stay there, and pursued him
when he came away. His family sent
news of the death of his great friend
Edward Ritz, and shortly afterwards
Goethe died. The French capital became
associated in his memory with moments
of great sorrow. In the final month of his

70

stay he suffered an attack of cholera. As soon as he had convalesced sufficiently, he left on the 8th of April, 1832, for London, where he had been invited for a series of concerts. On April 23 he was back in his rooms in Great Portland Street for a second visit, even happier than the first, so far as music and English friendships were concerned, but in May he received word that his old teacher Zelter was dead. He had been ill for some time, and Mendelssohn's letters indicate a premonition that he would not long survive Goethe, but the shock was no less severe when it occurred. On the 25th Mendelssohn tells his sister Fanny that the news came that morning just before a rehearsal of his Capriccio Brillante, and the applause and compliments of the musicians produced on him an ironic effect, far from their friendly intention; he was depressed by the sense that he was in a foreign land.

The second visit to England, therefore, had for him a double significance. The passing of his old friends marked for him certain important and not happy changes. Much of his later life would be spent in travel, but never again in such a carefree mood. In spite of his verdict on Paris, and allowing for minor disappointments, he had enjoyed until that spring of his twenty-third year phenomenal success. From now on the success would continue, but troubles of one kind or another would mar it.

The first of these darker experiences, directly connected with Zelter's death, we may speak of here, though the whole episode was completed only after Mendelssohn's return to Berlin. His father had written to him in

Paris that Zelter wanted him home to assist with the *Singakademie,* since if he didn't take up the directorship, someone else would. In reply Mendelssohn had asked whether Zelter expressed the wish that his pupil should succeed him, or whether the idea came from his father's imagination. The correct answer to that question we don't know, though it is reasonable enough to suppose that Zelter would have chosen Mendelssohn. But the family in Berlin and his friend Devrient were certain that Felix should offer himself at once as a candidate for the directorship, not only to satisfy his dead teacher's wishes but to save the *Singakademie* from falling into incompetent hands.

So long as he remained abroad, Mendelssohn took a very sane attitude; he reminded his father that the salary attaching to the post was small, and that even if he were wanted by the Berlin musicians, he could accept only for certain dates, as he had larger engagements to fill. Furthermore, if they wanted him, they would invite him. To offer himself as a candidate might prove embarrassing to all concerned.

On his return to Berlin, however, he was over-persuaded by his family and Devrient, became publicly a candidate for the directorship, and at the election was badly defeated, receiving only sixty votes out of two hundred and thirty-six. The defeat wounded his pride, and his family, who in this unfortunate exception were not wise, gave the episode a personal bearing which probably does not belong to it. One of his most recent biographers goes so far as to suggest that the *Singakademie* might have elected him if he hadn't been a Jew. This unnecessary interpretation would have been thought fanciful in days before the present world-orgy of prejudice, and the official honors later bestowed on Mendelssohn in Berlin suggest that race had nothing to do with the *Singakademie* election. The successful candidate was Karl Rungenhagen, a routine but amiable musician who had been Zelter's assistant, and whose promotion must have seemed to most members of the *Akademie* a matter of justice. Certainly Rungenhagen was no Mendelssohn, but he was known as a composer of four operas, three oratorios, and much other music, and at the time of his election he was a seasoned veteran of fifty-five. He would long ago have been forgotten, like his compositions, if he had not figured in this contest with a better man, but in his own day he was of consequence, and Mendelssohn's genius could hardly be as widely recognized in his twenty-fourth year as it is today.

Under Rungenhagen's leadership the *Singakademie* deteriorated and lost its importance. Mendelssohn would undoubtedly have insured for it a more brilliant career than it had even under Zelter, but as we can see now, and as he had foreseen in Paris, the task would have robbed him of hours needed for more important work.

But if the second London visit was saddened by the death of Zelter and by the first rumblings of the Berlin quarrel, it was made happy by the more than cordial reception Mendelssohn had from the London musicians. On

73

his arrival he dropped in one Saturday to a rehearsal of the Philharmonic. One of the players called out, "Here is Mendelssohn!" and he received an impromptu ovation. The "Hebrides" Overture was played from manuscript on May 14, and he was soloist in his own G minor Concerto on May 28 and June 18. On June 10 he played the organ at St. Paul's Cathedral, and shortly afterwards he published a four-hand arrangement of the *Midsummer Night's Dream* Overture, and the first book of the Songs Without Words. On this visit he made the acquaintance of William Horsley, a distinguished musician, father of gifted children, all remembered for achievements in music or painting. The Horsleys lived at Kensington, and Mendelssohn's letters show how deeply he prized their friendship and how much time he spent with them. By his own account few days passed without a meeting with some member of the family.

This London visit was short but crowded with important incidents, not the least of which was the publication of the first "Songs Without Words." Mendelssohn himself did not realize what these little pieces would contribute to his fame. He speaks almost with irritation of the trouble they gave him while he was preparing copy for the engraver. Apparently he did not appreciate the felicity of the name by which we now know them, "Lieder ohne Worte." The original English title was "Melodies for the Pianoforte."

To praise these masterpieces so late in the day is perhaps to annoy those who already know their worth and to exasperate those others for whom they are ruined by excessive familiarity or by inadequate performance. I gladly take both risks. The Songs Without Words are a remarkable contribution to music, and though their quality is uneven, it is unique. Other composers in Mendelssohn's time, his friends Chopin, Schumann, and Liszt, composed some of their best remembered things on a small scale, but Mendelssohn's Songs Without Words are different from anything else written in that period or since. Like the poet Tennyson, he suffered at the hands of those who copied him. If you no longer care for the Songs, perhaps it's not the concentrated originals but the diluted imitations that you have tired of.

The first book contained six Songs, the Andante con Moto in E major, the Andante Expressivo in A flat, the Hunting Song in A major, the well known Melody in the same key, the Presto Agitato in F sharp minor, and the best known of several Venetian Boat songs, that in G minor. They are all characteristically Mendelssohnian; they are written with extraordinary understanding of the piano, yet they suggest the singing voice. More than that, they incorporate in the melody the suggestion of words, yet they would be quite ruined if words were added.

The song quality of these pieces is self-evident, but their merit as compositions for the piano is less easy to recognize. Most amateurs have found to their grief that some of the Songs are technically difficult. The audience sometimes has cause to wish that the others were difficult too. Number Five in the first book, the Presto Agitato, calls for a nimbleness of finger and a control of touch quite beyond an incompetent pianist. For that reason the Presto is less familiar than the other five pieces.

We should remember that the piano in Mendelssohn's time, even the fine Erards which he found in England, had far less body of tone and singing quality than the concert instruments of our day, yet on the short-breathed pianos Mendelssohn, Chopin, Liszt, all in different styles, astonished their hearers by making the notes sing. This effect could be gained in part by lifting the damper pedal, but even when the pedal prolonged the tone, the sound prolonged would be a dying sound. The most practical way to make the piano sing is with the hand rather than the foot. Useful though the damper pedal is for certain glazing or binding effects, a note played with the right hand is best reinforced and sustained by the overtones or harmonics of a note or chord played in the left. You can investigate the phenomenon for yourself by a few simple experiments. Without using the pedal, strike and hold the note which singers call High C.

Now put your finger on the C an octave below, and press down gently so that the hammer will be lifted without hitting the string. Now play High C again and observe the increase in the length and power of the sound.

Now try the same experiment an octave lower, first pressing down the left hand, without hitting the strings, the triad on C. You will find that the note in the right hand is reinforced, but in addition the sustained chord constitutes a hand pedal for any note of that chord which the right hand may care to play.

These simple experiments make clearer the purpose of the running accompaniments which Mendelssohn so often employs in the Songs Without Words. The figures and patterns are not important of themselves, but they are essential supports for the melody. To get from them the maximum support, will call for considerable art in your piano playing. The very first of the Songs, usually considered by the novice easy, is a good example.

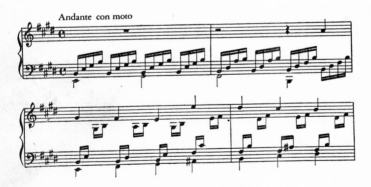

Obviously the chord in the left hand, or the melody doubled in the left hand, can produce effects of sonority,

77

even without a running accompaniment. In the Hunting Song and in the melody of Song No. 4 he employs octave-doublings and chord-doublings to produce something like a horn effect or an organ tone.

Have you ever thought much about the possible beauty of octaves? Composers for the orchestra usually know more about it than pianists, the unlucky pianists having dulled their ear by practicing scales one octave apart. But there's no law against playing scales two octaves apart, and the effect is lovely in the orchestra, and even on the piano, as Brahms well knew. Mendelssohn was one of the first to make extended use of such effects, and that he should have explored these possibilities while still very young, is a thing to marvel at.

Much more could be said about the essentially pianistic qualities of the Songs Without Words, but his profound knowledge of the instrument merely enabled him in these compositions to emphasize their special quality. If the Songs Without Words have an immense hold on music lovers everywhere, it is because of their unforgettable melodies, rather than the technical skill which helped to make those melodies unforgettable. The general music lover is interested in results, and magnificently indifferent to ways and means. For that reason the most popular of the six pieces in the first book is probably the Venetian Boat Song, a melody perfect in its kind, but now played by young amateurs so indefatigably that mature appreciation is a little numbed.

It is convenient to speak here of the Songs which followed in successive books, and which now form a single collection under one title. Book II was published in May, 1835, Book III in August, 1837, Book IV in May, 1841, Book V in April, 1844, Book VI in October, 1845, Book VII posthumously in February, 1851, Book VIII posthumously in June, 1868. This last book contains seven pieces. All the preceding books contain six. Many of the pieces were published separately before they were gathered into a group.

For the rest of his life, then, Mendelssohn continued to compose in this form which belongs to him. His songs for the piano vary in mood as he grows older, but less perhaps than one would expect. To the end he could write in the happy vein of his youth, witness the marvelous Spinning Song composed in 1843, four years before his death, or the well loved Spring Song, composed and badly played in 1842. The famous Melody of No. 3 in Book II is hardly less haunting than No. 2 of Book VIII. Mendelssohn's inspiration in these Songs was almost always unfailing and on a high level.

You and I will have our favorites among them. The three which I have most enjoyed playing and hearing are The Spinning Song, the Allegro non troppo, No. 2 in the third Book, and the Duet, No. 6 in the same collection.

The Allegro contains what I have always thought one of Mendelssohn's most beautiful melodies set to a superb accompaniment, apparently simple but full of varied and rich meanings. The Duet illustrates all of Mendelssohn's skill in making the piano sing, and all of his knowledge of piano registers. You should be able to hear in it, in clear contrast, the soprano and the baritone, questioning and answering and singing together.

CHAPTER EIGHT

Düsseldorf

MENDELSSOHN WAS IN BERLIN AGAIN by July, 1832. He made his third visit to England in April of the following year to act as godfather for the son of his friend Moscheles, and immediately afterwards he was in Düsseldorf rehearsing and conducting the Lower Rhine Festival, which began on May 26 and lasted three days. This schedule of constant travel, as he began to realize, was now his fate, unless he could find a permanent home, preferably in some large German city where he could exercise all his musical talents. He had found by experience that even while traveling he could compose and keep up his piano practice, but he wished an orchestra to conduct, choral groups with which to produce oratorios or cantatas, even, if possible, an opera company in which to give better performances than at that time could generally be found, and perhaps to produce operatic works of his own. His gifts and his ambitions took so many directions that the chances were against finding in any one place opportunity to develop them all. If the *Singakademie* election had gone in his favor, he might have looked forward to permanent residence in Berlin, but after his decisive defeat he felt that he must be a wanderer always, or at least be separated from his father's household. If there were no duties to detain him, he must travel wherever he and his art were wanted.

To a different nature this fate would have seemed normal and in no way tragic, but the Mendelssohn family were so closely bound to each other that any prolonged separation was painful. Felix and Fanny had shared each other's thoughts and dreams from childhood, in a companionship not often matched for mutual helpfulness. The father, Abraham Mendelssohn, had always been devoted to Felix, and now was more and more wrapped up in his son's career, promoting it with intelligence, except for the *Singakademie* episode. The realization that Felix must seek his fortune far away, saddened the older man, whose general health was failing, and who was threatened with blindness.

For all of these reasons, perhaps, Abraham Mendelssohn went to Düsseldorf to hear Felix rehearse and conduct the Festival, and after the Festival he accompanied him on a fourth visit to England. Abraham's letters to Berlin give us a charming picture of Düsseldorf and its Festival, and an invaluable portrait of Felix at this time. Though he had watched the young man conducting the Bach "Passion" four years before, and in recent months the *Walpurgis Nacht,* the *Midsummer Night's Dream* Overture and the "Hebrides" Overture, neither he nor any of the family had seen him take full responsibility for an important festival among strangers and potential critics. The letters home are rich in information for which the family then were eager, and we now are grateful.

Düsseldorf gave its Festival in a hall on the Berlin Road, a little over a mile from the town. The auditorium stood in a large tree-lined garden belonging to a restaurant, was a hundred and thirty-five feet long, seventy feet broad, and twenty-seven and a half feet high. Its walls were whitewashed. About one-third of the room was reserved for orchestra and chorus. The rest of the floor space was occupied by chairs numbered and fastened down. The audience of about thirteen hundred came from all the countryside for twenty miles or more, in every kind of conveyance, and the Düsseldorf authorities used their fire

83

engines to keep the road watered from the town to the concert hall.

The intermissions during the performance were at least half an hour, a longer pause, Abraham Mendelssohn says, than was usual in Berlin, but quite necessary for the Düsseldorf audience, whose habit was to rush into the garden, seat themselves at tables under the trees, and attack the landlord's supply of bread and butter, mineral water, beer, and May wine. Meanwhile the doors and windows of the concert room were thrown open for ventilation, and at the end of thirty minutes the brass in the orchestra blew a preliminary flourish which brought back most of the audience, and a second and louder fanfare, which even the hungriest and thirstiest obeyed.

In the chorus and orchestra there were about four hundred persons, admirable voices and admirable players, but until Felix Mendelssohn took hold of them, a bit casual and undisciplined both in rehearsals and in performance. Young though he was, Felix had the great conductor's authority and the talent for organization. His father was amused and perhaps not a little astonished to see the firmness with which he put an end to the orchestra's interminable tuning. Most of the men obeyed promptly his request that the maddening orgy be reduced to a minimum; when one or two forgot themselves, he rebuked them so sharply that there was no further trouble. He reformed the audience also. The Düsseldorf custom was to let the audience attend rehearsals, the difference between rehearsals and performances being chiefly that during the former the audience felt at liberty to come and go as they chose, and to carry on conversations, raising their voices to be heard above the music. If the conductor wished his instructions to be heard, he had to shout. Felix, having stopped the tuning in the orchestra, turned around and laid down the law to the talkers. Apparently he made his wishes known without giving offense. The Festival of 1833 was a model of good behavior, and the carefully prepared numbers went so well that orchestra, chorus, and audience were proud of themselves, and Felix became a popular hero.

The chief work performed at the Festival was Handel's *Israel in Egypt,* the success of which was magnificent. Other works were Beethoven's "Pastoral Symphony," the Overture to *Leonora,* and Mendelssohn's "Overture in C," the so-called "Trumpet" Overture, published later as Opus 101. After the final concert the music lovers of the city entertained Felix lavishly, and one excited young lady crowned him with a laurel wreath.

What was a more significant testimonial, however, came from the city, which invited him to be director of all its musical enterprises for a period of three years, at an annual salary of six hundred *thalers,* roughly the equivalent of five hundred dollars. Even if we allow for the high purchasing value of money a hundred years ago, the salary was small, and the position was one of somewhat doubtful authority. He himself says he was music director of the Association for the Promotion of Music in Düsseldorf, which seems not to have been an official body. Apparently his right to interfere with what the local musicians were already doing was to rest chiefly upon his prestige and his tact. With a good deal of enthusiasm, however, he accepted the appointment since it gave him, for a time at least, a settled opportunity. Promising to be back in Düsseldorf in September, he left with his father for London.

This stay repeated for Felix the happiness of the earlier visits, though it provided only informal opportunities for music. He played much among his friends, went into society, studied London itself, a city constantly more fascinating as his command of English improved. On one occasion he played the organ at St. Paul's. It wasn't service time, and the bellows' blowers were absent, but Klingemann and two other friends volunteered to pump while he improvised a prelude and fugue, and played considerable Bach. The church was quite empty, his father says, except for two ladies who stole in to listen. In the family letters there is much teasing about the London ladies and their love of music.

One memorable evening when Felix was detained in the country, his father dined with Klingemann, and afterwards attended a late party at Malibran's. The description which Abraham Mendelssohn wrote to his wife is often quoted as a picture of the kind of musical evening Felix constantly attended. The guests, most of them musicians, arrived about half-past ten, all prepared to entertain each other. First came a quartet of Haydn's, played very beautifully, though Abraham Mendelssohn feared he could detect some French taste in the interpretation. Then Madame Malibran sang simply and exquisitely what he describes as very dull sacred music. Then four of the guests sang a madrigal which Abraham thought thoroughly English, very queer, yet very pleasing.

At this point in the program Felix arrived, having returned from his out-of-town visit, and Madame Malibran sang a Spanish song, then at Felix's request two others, then an English sea song, and finally a French tambour-ditty. No words could describe, says the elder Mendelssohn, "with what flowing, glowing, and effervescing power and expression, what caprice and boldness, fashion and *esprit,* with what assurance and consciousness of her art, this woman, whom now I do appreciate, sang these songs. From the same throat issued Spanish passion, French coquetry with a touch of primitiveness, English unpolished soundness, and also that somewhat frivolous but fresh and most characteristic French audacity, and always with her own personality; she loved, yearned, rowed, and drummed with such wonderful self-possession, such bold command and lavish expenditure of her inexhaustible means, that one may truly say she sang songs without words, she sang sentiments, effects, situations. It was something quite new, and I wish you could have heard her! Felix, who justly or at any rate wisely refused to perform after her, was fetched by her from the adjoining room and forced to the piano. He extemporised to everybody's delight and my satisfaction on the airs she had just sung. After that she gave us two more Spanish songs, and lastly, with two daughters of the house, accompanied by Felix, the trio from the 'Matrimonio,' exquisitely!"

In the autumn Felix entered upon his duties at Düsseldorf. As it turned out, he was to spend not three but two years in the pleasant little city, but this short period was happy and fruitful. He was expected to oversee all the public concerts, to supervise and if possible improve the church music, and less directly to influence the performances at the opera house. The truth is that Düsseldorf was conscious of grave shortcomings in its music, and Felix had been selected as the necessary new broom. It is remarkable that he accomplished so much with so little antagonism from the musicians he superseded. He writes to his sister Rebecca, on October 26, 1833, that the church music had previously been under the direction of a crabbed old man whom the committee summoned before them in Felix's presence. We don't know what committee this was, but it makes little difference whether it represented a private organization or the city fathers; in either case the session would have been embarrassing. The old man must have been a sturdy type. He told his critics that he couldn't improve the music, and he wouldn't if he could, that if they wanted something better they must employ another man, that he didn't approve of the modern demand for beautiful music at all times—people weren't so unreasonable when he was young, and he thought he still played as well as ever. Mendelssohn says he was very reluctant to take the old man's place, though beyond question the music needed mending. "I couldn't help thinking how I'd feel were *I* to be summoned, some fifty years hence, to Town Hall, and spoken to in this strain, and a young green-horn snubbed me, and my coat was seedy, and I hadn't the remotest idea why the music should suddenly be better. I felt rather uncomfortable."

The church choirs apparently had no good music in their collections. Mendelssohn at once took a coach to Elberfeld, Bonn, and Cologne, searched the music stores and libraries, and brought back the Misereres of Allegri and Bai, the Motets of Orlando Lasso, Pergolesi, and Palestrina. This music obviously was intended for the churches of a Catholic city. Mendelssohn, though not a Catholic himself, and in spite of his love of Bach, entered into this part of his Düsseldorf task with enthusiasm, expressing the conviction that true church music was possible only in liturgical services. Many another musician has since rediscovered the same fact.

In addition to church music, symphonic concerts, and opera performances, Mendelssohn was charged with the program for special civic occasions, such as the entertainment organized for the Crown Prince when he visited Düsseldorf, an elaborate affair, hardly worthy of his time and effort. Felix gives an account of the ceremony in a letter to his sister Rebecca, October 26, 1833.

"I must now describe to you the fête that was given in his honor, and for which I suggested the employment of some old transparencies, to be connected, by appropriate verses for 'Israel in Egypt,' with *tableaux vivants*. They took place in the great Hall of the Academy, where a stage was erected. In front was the double chorus (about ninety voices altogether), standing in two semicircles round my English piano; and in the room seats for four hundred spectators. R——, in medieval costume, interpreted the whole affair, and contrived very cleverly, in iambics, to combine the different objects, in spite of their disparity.

"He exhibited three transparencies:—first, 'Melancholy,' after Dürer, a motet of Lotti's being given by men's voices in the far distance; then the Raphael, with the Virgin appearing to him in a vision, to which the 'O Sanctissima' was sung (a well-known song, but which always makes people cry); thirdly, St. Jerome in his tent, with a song of Weber's 'Hör' uns, Wahrheit.' This was the first part. Now came the best of all. We began from the very beginning of 'Israel in Egypt.' Of course you know the first recitative, and how the chorus gradually swells in tone; first the voices of the *alti* are heard alone, then more voices join in, till the loud passage comes with single chords, 'They sighed,' etc. (in G minor), when the curtain rose, and displayed the first tableau, 'The Children of Israel in bondage,' designed and arranged by Bendemann. In the foreground was Moses, gazing dreamily into the distance in sorrowful apathy; beside him an old man sinking to the ground under the weight of a beam, while his son makes an effort to relieve him from it; in the background some beautiful figures with uplifted arms, a few weeping children in the foreground—

the whole scene closely crowded together like a mass of fugitives. This remained visible till the close of the first chorus; and when it ended in C minor, the curtain at the same moment dropped over the bright picture. A finer effect I scarcely ever saw.

"The chorus then sang the plagues, hail, darkness, and the first-born, without any tableau; but at the chorus, 'He led them through like sheep,' the curtain rose again, when Moses was seen in the foreground with raised staff, and behind him, in gay tumult, the same figures who in the first tableau were mourning, now all pressing onwards, laden with gold and silver vessels; one young girl (also by Bendemann) was especially lovely, who, with her pilgrim's staff, seemed as if advancing from the side scenes and about to cross the stage. Then came the choruses again, without any tableau, 'But the waters,' 'He rebuked the Red Sea,' 'Thy right hand, O Lord,' and the recitative, 'And Miriam, the Prophetess,' at the close of which the solo soprano appeared. At the same moment the last tableau was uncovered,—Miriam, with a silver timbrel, sounding praises to the Lord, and other maidens with harps and citherns, and in the background four men with trombones, pointing in different directions. The soprano solo was sung behind the scene, as if proceeding from the picture; and when the chorus came in *forte,* real trombones, and trumpets, and kettle-drums, were brought on the stage, and burst in like a thunderclap. Handel evidently intended this effect, for after the commencement he makes them pause till they come in again in C major, when the other instruments recommence. And thus we concluded the second part.

"This last tableau was by Hübner, and pleased me exceedingly. The effect of the whole was wonderfully fine. Much might possibly have been said against it had it been a pretentious affair, but its character was entirely social, and not public, and I think it would scarcely be possible to devise a more charming fête. The next that followed was a *tableau vivant,* designed and arranged by Schadow, 'Lorenzo de' Medici, surrounded by the Geniuses of Poetry, Sculpture, and Painting, leading to him Dante, Raphael, Michael Angelo, and Bramante,' with a complimentary allusion to the Crown Prince, and a final chorus. The second division consisted of the comic scenes from the 'Midsummer Night's Dream,' represented by the painters here; but I did not care so much for it, having been so absorbed by the previous one."

The musicians with whom Mendelssohn accomplished good results at Düsseldorf were not in any modern sense professionals. Both singers and orchestra players earned their living as workmen, shopkeepers or farmers, or were occupied in ordinary housekeeping. The district was full of natural talent, but the standards of performance must have been very low. The Mendelssohn letters refer to the stiff fingers of the violinists, or to the stiff lips of the woodwind players. In the sounds emanating from the chorus any ear, even moderately acute, could detect differences of opinion as to how a tone should be produced or a word pronounced.

This amateurish condition must be remembered if we are to appreciate the results which Mendelssohn in a very short time achieved. What had fascinated Düsseldorf when he conducted the Lower Rhine Festival was his rare gift for disentangling such confusion. He must have been a rare teacher. Even during the brief Festival he inspired the orchestra to play so well that they hardly recognized themselves, and he gave the chorus the specific instruction they needed to cover up their worst defects. During his permanent engagement at Düsseldorf he continued this progress until, when he left the city, he had established the tradition of professional quality in performance.

This kind of success can be accurately measured only by those who are present to witness the change, and for that reason we are likely to overlook one talent of Mendelssohn's which conferred immense benefit on the music of modern Germany and of the modern world. Not only did he further the appreciation of Sebastian Bach and other classics, but he set the standard of orchestral playing and choral singing as high as Liszt set the standard of piano playing. After his service at Düsseldorf—even more, after his career at Leipzig—German music acquired its reputation for its professional craftsmanship rather than for the amiable folk quality of semi-amateur good will. Hearty and unsubtle singing or playing, even when perpetrated in the comfortable neighborhood of the beer garden, could no longer satisfy the public once the austere masters like Bach were adequately presented. After Mendelssohn had electrified Düsseldorf with the *Israel in*

Egypt, or taught the city to like Palestrina, the modern art of music had a public taste and a public conscience to appeal to.

So far as opera was concerned, Düsseldorf started at the bottom, and if Mendelssohn had known the difficulties of opera production, he might not have put himself to the test in this field. But he still believed he had it in him to be a composer for the theatre, and Düsseldorf was the home of Karl Immermann, the poet friend who had promised to furnish him with a libretto. In fact, the libretto had already been forthcoming, and Mendelssohn was so dissatisfied with it that he let the matter drop, but his general confidence in Immermann remained and he joined with him in forming a theatrical association which was to produce both plays and operas, Immermann directing the plays, Mendelssohn taking entire charge of the operas.

It is hard to imagine how any human being could carry such a program—orchestra rehearsals and concerts, choir and choral rehearsals, public ceremonies, constant composing and piano playing, and the complete management of an opera company, engaging and training the stars, teaching them to act as well as to sing, directing the stage, and at the performance conducting the orchestra. For a short time this is what Mendelssohn undertook. He and Immermann got off to a bad start by describing their first production as "classical." Just why that name should offend the citizens of Düsseldorf is not clear. Perhaps the major part of the offense lay in the high price for tickets

94

which the joint directors, poet and composer, thought necessary in order to improve the production. In any case the audience came in an ugly mood and broke up the performance in a small riot. On second thought, however, the rioters were ashamed of themselves, and those who remained impenitent were disciplined by the civil authorities. *Don Giovanni* was repeated with great success, and other operas followed, among them the *Nozze di Figaro, Oberon, Freischutz,* all enthusiastically received.

But the theatre was not Mendelssohn's proper world, reluctant though he was to admit the fact. He soon grew tired of the jealousies between artists, of the complaints from the orchestra, of the necessity to teach their parts, note by note, to singers who had a voice and could act but didn't know how to read music. When he sat down to compose in the morning, he says, the doorbell rang at every other bar. In self-defense he resigned his opera tasks, accepting a merely honorary post and surrendering part of his salary to the director who succeeded him. But of course, whether or not his position was now called honorary, he was still called upon for aid and suggestions. In his letter of November 4, 1834, he tells his mother that he had at last severed all connection, even honorary, with the Düsseldorf theatre. Immermann was disappointed, and the friendship was decidedly strained, but the citizens of Düsseldorf understood his point of view and remained his devoted admirers.

Having put the opera house out of his life, he turned

seriously to the composing of oratorios, and began work on his own *St. Paul.*

In the spring of 1834 he was greatly pleased by election to the Berlin Academy of Fine Arts. The honor seemed to him in some measure an atonement for whatever wrong had been done to him by the *Singakademie,* and the memory of that unpleasant episode began to fade. About the same time, in May, he attended the Lower Rhine Festival, given this year at Aix-la-Chapelle and conducted by Ferdinand Ries. One of the works performed was Handel's *Deborah,* with additional orchestral parts written for this occasion by Ferdinand Hiller, who came from Paris and brought Chopin along. Mendelssohn attended, no doubt to hear the music, but also to renew his acquaintance with old friends. The three lived together, had a private box in the theatre, and spent their mornings at the piano. Mendelssohn wrote to his mother that as a pianist Chopin had improved to a point where he was now in the very first rank. "He produces new effects, like Paganini on his violin, and accomplishes wonderful passages such as no one could formerly have thought practical." Both Hiller and Chopin, he said, played in a spasmodic and impassioned style which too often took liberties with the tempo, but he admitted that perhaps he himself erred on the other side. He never cared for the free rhythms of Chopin, his taste remained strictly classical, yet even though he disagreed he was fascinated, and he persuaded Chopin and Hiller to ride back with him to Düsseldorf, where they spent another day in piano playing and discussion. On their journey back to Paris he accompanied them as far as Cologne.

The Düsseldorf days were happy, but they were only an interlude between youthful study and travels and mature accomplishments. Early in 1835 Mendelssohn was invited to be conductor of the Gewandhaus concerts in Leipzig. He went to his new post in September.

CHAPTER NINE

Leipzig

BEFORE MENDELSSOHN WENT TO LEIP-
zig he once more conducted the Lower
Rhine Festival, this time at Cologne,
June 7 to 9, 1835. Among other things
he presented Handel's *Solomon,* with
an additional organ part which he had
composed while in Italy. His success in
these performances was as usual very
great, and his pleasure in them was increased by the presence of both his par-

ents. The family letters show how closely his father, though in failing health, followed in every detail the planning and preparation of the performances. At the close Felix received from the Cologne musicians a handsome gift which remained for him a permanent delight— a complete set of Handel's works in thirty-two folio volumes bound in thick green leather, inscribed "To Director F.M.B. from the Committee of the Cologne Musical Festival, 1835." The very first time he opened the volumes he found, he said, an aria for *Samson,* until then quite unknown, and immediately he began planning performances of undiscovered Handel material.

Returning to Berlin with his parents he stayed until the end of August, troubled by the illness now of his mother as well as his father. When he said good-bye at last, it was with a presentiment that he might not see them again. In October he was able to visit them for two days, but on November 19, 1835, Abraham Mendelssohn died suddenly. Felix began his Leipzig experiences without the loving advice which had always guided him.

Leipzig at the moment was one of the most interesting musical centers in Europe. Mendelssohn added so much to its fame that we must remind ourselves of what the city did for him. The Gewandhaus concerts which he made famous had been established in Sebastian Bach's time. They had first been given in a private house, from 1743 on, with a small orchestra of sixteen. After 1763 the orchestra was doubled, and in 1781 the concerts were transferred to the Gewandhaus, the old market hall of the linen merchants, and their support was guaranteed by subscription, chiefly through the efforts of the music loving Burgermeister, Karl Wilhelm Müller. The programs were symphonic and choral, with occasional vocal or instrumental solos. After 1809 a chamber music series was added. The Gewandhaus concerts continue to this day in the beautiful modern hall, opened in 1884, where many of the finest performances in the history of German music have been given. The glory of the Gewandhaus, however, is a legend of Mendelssohn's conducting.

The fact alone that Sebastian Bach had been organist at St. Thomas's would have made Leipzig attractive to Mendelssohn, but when he began his duties there he was associated immediately with Friedrich Wieck, the famous piano teacher, with Clara Wieck, his daughter, and of course with Robert Schumann, already publishing his critical articles as leader in the new romantic movement. Clara Wieck played the Beethoven B flat Trio at Mendelssohn's first Gewandhaus concert, and the day before, Felix met Schumann at Friedrich Wieck's house. Moscheles came from London to join him, and other musical friends gathered promptly as though they realized the importance of what would now be heard in Leipzig. Chopin, whose playing Mendelssohn admired more and more, though he remained less enthusiastic about his music, came from Paris, and played for him some new études, one of his concertos, and a new nocturne. Mendelssohn played over for him his oratorio, *St. Paul*.

Besides these and other musical friends, all most stimulating, Mendelssohn found in Leipzig an excellent orchestra, proud of its tradition and on the whole well trained. He said its best quality was the high musical intelligence of its players, which enabled them to receive his suggestions quickly. In a very short time it became the best orchestra in Germany, perhaps the best in Europe, or even the best at that time in the world.

There were to be twenty concerts a season and certain extra concerts, the number of which might vary.

At the first concert Mendelssohn played his own "Meeresstille" (Calm Sea) Overture and the Fourth Symphony of Beethoven. The acoustics of the hall were admirable, and the audience listened attentively to the most delicate effects. On the other hand the orchestra attacked loud and brilliant passages with such vitality that the young conductor says he was startled as well as delighted. He had probably never heard such orchestral playing before. Besides his Overture and Beethoven's Symphony, there was a violin concerto by Spohr, and minor pieces.

The audience was surprised, not all of them at first pleased, by what was then an innovation. Hitherto orchestra conducting had traditionally been a matter of collaboration between the conductor and the leader of the first violins, who for that reason was called the concertmeister. The concertmeister played standing up, and the conductor sat at a harpsichord or piano, signaling to the concertmeister whatever he wished the orchestra to do. At Mendelssohn's first Leipzig concert the concertmeister was seated in the modern way, at the head of the violin section, setting the example for entrances and bowing. Mendelssohn stood up and conducted with hands and baton.

At the second concert Moscheles played Mendelssohn's Piano Concerto, and at the chamber music concert Moscheles, Clara Wieck, and Mendelssohn played Bach's Triple Concerto in D minor. Familiar as all this music now is, it was then either new or long neglected. The Gewandhaus concerts became opportunities not only to hear a superb orchestra, but to make the acquaintance of great compositions.

The success of the Gewandhaus concerts was from the very beginning so unmistakable, and their reputation grew so steadily, that we are tempted to claim for Mendelssohn greater conducting talent than perhaps he possessed. In our day, when the virtuoso conductor often means more to the public than the artists themselves, the biographer hesitates to discourage Mendelssohn's admirers by recording the fact that his genius was essentially creative, and that the Leipzig concerts were glorified by imagination, insight, and Promethean fire rather than by consummate skill with the baton. From what his friendliest critics said of him we gather that in the actual concerts his intense vitality swept orchestra and audience along with him, yet in technical matters his conducting was not always dependable. His letters and other testimony indicate that some of the finest performances over which he presided were marred by slight mishaps. He

was always an artist of the highest conscience, asking perfection from others as well as from himself, but in moments of excitement he had less than complete control of
his men. He probably was aware of this shortcoming. The
audience kindled at the sight of his platform liveliness,
but the players were at times baffled by it, great as was
their personal devotion to him.

At Leipzig after a few moments he strengthened the
orchestra by securing as concertmeister his friend Ferdinand David, one of the greatest violinists of his time.
David, his junior by a year, a native of Hamburg, had
studied under Spohr, and had made Mendelssohn's acquaintance in 1827 and 1828 while playing in the orchestra of the Koenigstadt Theatre, Berlin. From 1829 to
1835 he toured the principal cities of Russia, and was a
well-established artist when Mendelssohn persuaded him
to accept the Leipzig post. From that moment the quality
of the Gewandhaus concerts was secure, David providing
the steadiness that was lacking, and contributing, by his
own art and by his influence upon the other players to the
imaginative and dramatic effects which Mendelssohn
sought. From 1838 on, David guided Mendelssohn in the
composition of the Violin Concerto in E, and he was the
soloist at its first performance at the Gewandhaus concert
on March 13, 1845.

The vision and the good sense by which Mendelssohn
built up his orchestra, inspired also the choice of his
Leipzig programs. Not only did he perform neglected
masterpieces and introduce new compositions, but with

statesman-like tact he advanced the cause of music, even on occasions when he might have been pardoned if he had let the opportunity pass by. When Liszt, in one of his more egotistic moments, came to Leipzig on a concert tour in 1840, and offended the city by the exorbitant price of his tickets, Mendelssohn immediately arranged a special concert at the Gewandhaus in which Liszt appeared to such advantage that he became popular again. At no time had Mendelssohn received just appreciation in France, and he reciprocated by doubting the value of contemporary French music, but in 1843, when Berlioz came to Leipzig, a Gewandhaus program was devoted to the visitor's compositions. Liszt was too valuable to music not to be saved, and Berlioz, though Mendelssohn was less sure of him, was contributing to art something new and vital, and therefore must be heard.

Mendelssohn's duties in Leipzig did not prevent him from conducting elsewhere, and he continued in demand at the numerous German Festivals. On May 22, 1836, the Oratorio *St. Paul* was given at the Lower Rhine Festival at Düsseldorf, and during the illness of Johann Schelble, the distinguished conductor of the Caecilian Society of Frankfurt, Mendelssohn took his place. The Frankfurt visit lasted six weeks, and for more than one reason proved enjoyable. Hiller was living there, Rossini was passing through; they and other musicians formed a circle in which Mendelssohn was as usual the dominating personality.

And in Frankfurt he met Cécile Charlotte Sophie Jeanrenaud, his future wife. He was then twenty-seven, she nearly ten years younger, a beautiful girl of French descent. In September their engagement was announced, and they were married in Frankfurt early the following year, March 28, 1837.

Fortunate as Mendelssohn was, he was happier in nothing than in his marriage. His wife was his ideal mate, sharing naturally his ideals and his tastes, and though not like him a genius, yet endowed with the intelligence, the intuitions, and the forbearance which are needed to get on with one. They had five children, Karl, Marie, Paul, Felix, and Elisabeth. Felix died in infancy; the others enjoyed the beautiful understanding with their parents which had characterized generations of Mendelssohns.

The climax of Mendelssohn's achievements in Leipzig was the foundation of the famous Conservatory. Though the project did not take shape until the end of his life, he began to think of it in his earliest Gewandhaus years. He had always been a missionary for the immortal things of his beloved art, and Germany needed, he was convinced, more gospel-spreading in a more permanent form. Perhaps his association with David, who was not only a great player but also a great teacher, turned his thoughts directly to the problem of musical education. Undoubtedly his experience with the amateur or semi-amateur orchestras at the Lower Rhine Festivals, and with the conditions he found even in so good an organization as the Frankfurt Caecilian Society, impressed upon him the need of widely distributed professional craftsmanship if

German music were to accomplish as much as the national talent promised.

His own direct contacts with the problem of education were from some points of view slight, and his personal experience was, as he knew, not typical; he had grown up in a remarkable family where history, philosophy, literature, and the arts were constant preoccupations, and any formal instruction had come from private tutors. His acquaintance with the system of public education had been made through his brief attendance at the University of Berlin, and through the honorary doctorate in philosophy which the University of Leipzig bestowed on him in 1836. Yet he had grasped certain principles which are not yet universally understood. He knew that study with private tutors, a privilege reserved for the wealthy, is sometimes not a privilege at all but a serious hazard, since it deprives the student of the companionship of other students and of the resulting cross-fertilization of mind which not even genius can do without. In music the disadvantages of private study are formidable. It is possible to master one or more instruments with different teachers, and to acquire with others a knowledge of harmony and counterpoint, of orchestration and conducting, and once this equipment is drawn from various sources, it is possible for a strong talent to amalgamate the results. But in a conservatory properly staffed all subjects can be pursued under great artists, who confer over the needs of each pupil, and the pupils inspire each other.

On the same principle the ideal conservatory should by

its location be associated with other important educational institutions, with museums and libraries, and should be in the neighborhood of the best concerts. A school which hopes to influence the life of a nation should have its place in the stream of that national life, in a large city rather than a small town, as near as possible to the intellectual frontier.

These educational ideals Mendelssohn stated once for all in a letter to the Home Minister of Saxony April 8, 1840. This document, both in its eventual results for Leipzig and in the vision it provides for later musical education elsewhere, is as important as any single masterpiece which Mendelssohn composed. The Paris Conservatoire, founded by the inspired patriots of the French Revolution, illustrated of course the same ideals, but Mendelssohn's influence in the world carried his famous letter beyond national boundaries.

He asked the Home Minister whether a legacy which the State had recently received for the purpose of establishing a school for art and science might not be used to found and maintain a school of music in Leipzig.

"Permit me to make a few observations on the importance of such an institution, and to state why I consider Leipzig peculiarly entitled to aspire to such a one, and also what I consider to be the fitting basis for its organization.

"For a long period music has been indigenous in this country, and the sense of what is true and genuine, the very phase which must be nearest the heart of every ardent and thoughtful friend to art, has at all times struck its roots deep into this soil. Such universal sympathy certainly does not come by chance, nor is it without influential results on general cultivation; music having thus become an important power, not as a mere passing enjoyment, but as a more elevated and intellectual requirement. Those who feel sincere solicitude about this art must eagerly wish that its future prospects in this land should rest on the most solid foundation.

"The positive, technical, and material tendencies so prevalent at the present day render the preservation of a genuine sense of art, and its further advancement, of twofold importance, but also of twofold difficulty. A solid basis alone can accomplish this purpose; and as the extension of sound instruction is the best mode of promoting every species of moral improvement, so it is with music also. If we had a good music academy—embracing all the various branches of this art, and teaching them from one sole point of view, as only the means to a higher end—then the practical and material tenets, which, alas! can number even among our artists many influential adherents, might, no doubt, yet be effectually checked.

"Mere private instruction which once bore much good fruit for the world at large, on many accounts now no longer suffices. Formerly, students of various instruments were to be found in every class of society, whereas now this amateurship is gradually passing away, or is chiefly confined to one instrument—the piano.

"Scholars desirous of enjoying further instruction always invariably consist of those who propose devoting themselves to this branch of art, and who rarely possess the means of paying for private lessons. The most admirable talent is indeed often to be found amongst this class; but, on the other hand, teachers are seldom placed in such fortunate circumstances as to be able to devote their time, without remuneration, to the training of even the finest genius; thus both sides endure privation—the former being unable to obtain the wished-for instruction, and the latter losing the opportunity of implanting, and practically enforcing, their own knowledge. A public institution would, at this moment, be of the most vital importance to teachers as well as to pupils; and the latter would thus acquire the means of improving capabilities which otherwise must often remain undeveloped and wasted; while, for the teachers of music, such a standard of combined action from *one* point of view, and for the attainment of *one* purpose, would also be advantageous, as the best remedy against lukewarmness and isolation, the unfruitfulness of which, in these days, is but too apt to exercise a ruinous influence on the mind.

"In Leipzig the need of a school for music, in which Art may be pursued with conscientious study and an earnest mind, is deeply felt; and for various reasons Leipzig seems peculiarly suited for it. The university is already a central locality for intellectual aspiring young men, and the school of knowledge would, in many relations, connect itself with the school of music. In most of the other large towns of Germany public amusements dissipate the mind, and exercise an injurious influence over the young; here, however, most of these amusements are more or less connected with music, or consist wholly of it; thus there are very few public recreations except those allied to music; so this institution would benefit both the cause and the individual; moreover, for that especial branch of art which must always remain the chief basis of musical studies—the more elevated class of instrumental and sacred compositions—Leipzig, by its very numerous concerts and oratorios, possesses the means of cultivating the taste of young artists to an extent that few other German cities can offer."

The legacy with which Mendelssohn proposed to establish a conservatory amounted to no more than 20,000 *thalers,* but the King of Saxony supplemented this endowment from his private purse. In November, 1842, the corporation of the town granted permission to use necessary rooms in the Gewandhaus, and on April 3, 1843, the Leipzig Conservatory began its distinguished career with a remarkable faculty. Mendelssohn was the Director. He and Robert Schumann taught composition and piano. Mauritz Hauptmann, the Cantor of the ancient Thomasschule, was professor of harmony and counterpoint. Ferdinand David taught violin. Christian August Pohlenz, a former Cantor of the Thomasschule, was chosen to teach singing, but he died before classes began. Carl Ferdinand Becker, organist of the Nikolaikirche in Leipzig, was professor of organ. In 1846 Mendelssohn persuaded Moscheles to leave London and join the Conservatory's piano department.

Mendelssohn was an excellent teacher. In the piano class he had half a dozen pupils, whom he taught together twice a week for a period of two hours. The composition class met once a week for the same length of time, each pupil bringing in a composition to be heard and criticized in the presence of the others. As for the time spent on executive duty as head of the school, we have eloquent testimony in the orderly records of pupil-attendance with comments on their abilities and their progress, all in Mendelssohn's handwriting. How he found leisure for composition is incomprehensible.

CHAPTER TEN

St. Paul and the Hymn of Praise

To THESE LEIPZIG YEARS BELONG A
large group of important compositions,
some of which are discussed in later
chapters. Here it is appropriate to speak
of Mendelssohn's choral writing. It was
at Leipzig that he completed his *St.
Paul* and the "Lobgesang" (*Hymn of
Praise*), and began his greatest oratorio,
Elijah.

St. Paul had been suggested to Men-

delssohn by his father, who believed Felix was des-
tined to carry on the tradition of German religious music,
with Sebastian Bach for his model. Doubtless Mendelssohn would have carried out his father's wish even if he
had stayed in Düsseldorf, but in Leipzig the spirit of
Bach, still a reality in St. Thomas's Church, in the
Thomasschule, in practically all the musical organizations
of the city, inevitably induced the composing of further
oratorios and cantatas.

Mendelssohn was by temperament deeply religious.
Whether or not the strictly orthodox would have ap-
proved, his breadth of mind and his emotional sympathy
drew him to all faiths. With the tolerance characteristic
of all his family, he took pains to understand Catholicism,
so far as this was possible for a non-Catholic, and though
he and his people no longer practiced the Jewish rituals
of their fathers, at least he gave his heart, in German
Protestantism, to those ideals of practical conduct and
to that piety of the home which Judaism emphasizes.
Between German Protestantism and the Jewish philosophy
there were remarkable affinities, the same insistence on
good works, the same respect for prosperity and success,
the same integrity and moral devotion.

One reason, no doubt, for Mendelssohn's distrust of
France and his love of England was that among the English alone he found the underlying religious sentiment,
the preoccupation with church music and the quickness to
understand Sebastian Bach, which characterized German
Protestantism. To this day in England Mendelssohn's

oratorios enjoy a popularity not equalled in other countries, and though their reputation everywhere is high, we
should perhaps recognize the fact that it rests almost as
much on religious as on musical grounds.

The composition of *St. Paul* cost Mendelssohn an
unusual effort. For once his inspiration did not flow
freely. Since the work is ranked nowadays below *The
Hymn of Praise* and *Elijah,* we sometimes explain its
comparative failure by a temporary decline of his powers.
Yet *St. Paul* is a failure only in parts. Individual numbers are very fine indeed. Perhaps we may put it another
way; it is a failure just so far as we can enjoy it piece by
piece. It lacks a central idea. The worst kind of plot,
Aristotle warned us, is that which tries to secure unity
by the mere recital of all that happened to one man.

Mendelssohn himself gathered and arranged the materials of his libretto. His correspondence shows that he
was grateful for the advice of Pastor Julius Schubring and
other friends, but the book of his oratorio was his own
work, and from it we can understand why he never wrote
an important opera.

Religious emotion naturally expresses itself, like any
other emotion, lyrically, but there is a drama of feelings
as well as of actions, and a successful oratorio, like a successful opera must be—at least in the emotional sense—
dramatic. Although Mendelssohn could be dramatic
enough in his music, when the music stood by itself, the
text for the *St. Paul* illustrates the extent to which
words got in his way. The martyrdom of St. Stephen and

the conversion of St. Paul are materials for drama, but Mendelssohn tried to convey it by a narrative text set to dramatic music, as though emotion could be conferred upon the words. The fifth number of Part I, for example, is the chorus, "Now this man ceaseth not to utter blasphemous words against the law of Moses and also God. Did we not enjoin and straitly command you that ye should not teach in the name ye follow?" Anyone who has sung this chorus will recall the fugue which begins, "Did we not enjoin and straitly command you." The fugue is dramatic but the words are not, and it's perhaps an advantage that as soon as the voices begin answering each other contrapuntally, we can't tell what they are saying.

Mendelssohn's arrangement of Biblical quotations quite as much as his choice of them, shows that he was neither a playwright nor a story-teller. Stephen, the first martyr, was stoned for his faith in Christ, but unless more is told of him than this, his tragic fate is only potentially dramatic. You can't make a play out of a lynching unless you tell much more about the victim than that he was lynched.

The conversion of St. Paul, which we should expect to be the main episode, is recited with startling brevity in a dialogue between tenor and bass, and a few measures of chorus. The second part of the oratorio recounts St. Paul's miraculous work and his departure from Ephesus.

If the reader cares to pursue these ideas further into the whole problem of setting words to music, he may profitably compare Mendelssohn's letters referring to *St. Paul*, with the correspondence between Richard Strauss and Hugo von Hofmannstahl, an exchange of significant ideas between a great composer and his librettist, a skilful poet and dramatist. Mendelssohn dealt with his text as though it were final, partly because he had found it in the Bible but quite as much, perhaps, because he didn't know how to adapt it to music. Strauss and von Hofmannstahl understood the subtle adjustments both of words and of music which must be devised before the two can be put together.

Following Sebastian Bach's example, Mendelssohn inserted in his oratorio a number of German chorales. Some of his friends advised him not to do this, but he followed his own instinct and undoubtedly was right. The chorales sustain the religious mood, without which the oratorio would be much less effective. The fine old hymns, noble words to well-fitted music, provide thoroughly satisfying moments, and bind together the whole work as much as a composition so loose-jointed could be unified.

What keeps *St. Paul* alive is the beauty of the choruses, especially in certain lyrical numbers, which at their best are true Mendelssohn. They are written with such understanding of the voice that their beauty is realized only when they are sung. The opening chorus, "Lord, Thou alone art God," may not astonish you if you merely play it over on the piano, but if you can hear it well sung and not feel some pleasant chills down your spine, your nervous system needs investigating. Probably the most perfect chorus in the whole work is the gentle, "Happy and blessed are they," with its stately theme, its graceful accompaniment, its lovely pianissimo ending, and its serene postlude. But singers often prefer the elaborate and slightly pompous, "Rise up, arise," perhaps because of the great chorale, "Sleepers wake," which is its climax. To the present writer the finest writing next after "Happy and blessed are they," is in Number 22, "O great is the depth," the chorus which concludes the first part of the oratorio.

The solos in *St. Paul* are inferior and are now rarely heard with the exception of Number 13, the contralto aria "But the Lord is mindful of His own." In spite of its once great popularity, most of us now find it over-saccharine.

From the second part the duet between tenor and bass, "Now we are ambassadors," is still rendered in church services, usually serving, as Mendelssohn intended, for prelude to the chorus which immediately follows, "How lovely are the messengers." The duet is pleasantly amiable and mercifully short, so that we are not completely bored by the two voices singing in thirds. The famous chorus, with its cheerful, almost jaunty, theme, still delights those who can enjoy the music without attending to the words, but the judicious are likely to be puzzled or offended by the disparity between the religious ecstasy of the text and the casualness of the merry tune.

For an understanding of Mendelssohn, of his character as well as his genius, a more careful study of the *St.*

Paul than we can give it here would be profitable. The family letters written during its composition and after each early performance of it, indicate that he was feeling his way into a field which attracted him deeply, but in which he did not feel at home. He toiled conscientiously over this work but he was not satisfied with the result. Any attempt to give a just estimate of his place in music must notice the limitations of his talent, but must also stress the clear judgment and the splendid humility with which he measured what he had done, and went on to better things. *St. Paul* was a preliminary exercise for *Elijah* and for the intermediate cantatas. In this kind of writing he never acquired the facility which by nature he had for instrumental music, but by determined study he made rapid advance, as he demonstrated at the Leipzig Gutenberg Festival, held in June, 1840, to commemorate the invention of printing.

For this occasion Mendelssohn composed two choral works, the "Festgesang" and the "Lobgesang" (*The Hymn of Praise*). The "Festgesang" is a brief cantata for male chorus and brass band, a rather noisy piece, presented out of doors in the Leipzig market place on June 24. Mendelssohn wrote his mother that there were over two hundred men in the chorus; in the band there were twenty trombones, sixteen trumpets, and the rest of the instrumentation in proportion. For antiphonal effects chorus and orchestra were divided, Mendelssohn conducting one group, David the other, so far apart that Mendelssohn says there must have been a hundred yards between them.

Whatever the distance, it was enough to make team-play difficult, but the two conductors by all accounts kept together, and the Festival began in a mood of enthusiasm.

Since the "Festgesang" was designed for the occasion and the condition of its first performance, there would be little reason to repeat it under other circumstances. Its effects are obtained on a large scale, without subtlety, and for a satisfactory performance it needs space, but the treatment of voices and band was well adapted to its purpose. By a curious consequence of Mendelssohn's English popularity, the music of the second number is now the only part of the "Festgesang" which is familiar, all because William Hayman Cummings, organist of Waltham Abbey and later known as a singer, adapted it to Charles Wesley's Christmas hymn, "Hark, the Herald Angels Sing." Listening to the popular melody, few of us realize that Mendelssohn composed it to celebrate, not the manger in Bethlehem, but Gutenberg's printing press.

The Hymn of Praise was performed on June 25 in St. Thomas's Church. This lovely work, of an entirely different order from the "Festgesang" and immensely superior to the *St. Paul,* is what Mendelssohn called a symphony cantata, the orchestral part being more important than a mere accompaniment, and the whole having a certain unity, or at least continuity. The different sections are set off by changes of tempo and theme, but the total impression is precisely what the title indicates, a song-like mood of thanksgiving. Mendelssohn chose the text himself, so far as we know, without aid or advice. Except for a famous chorale, "Nun danket alle Gott," the words are taken from the Psalms, and the music fits perfectly the lyrical text.

The opening chorus, "All men, all things," continues without a pause into the soprano solo, "Praise thou the Lord, O my spirit." Throughout this second number the solo voice alternates with a female chorus. Again without a pause we go on to the tenor recitative, "Sing ye praise," and the aria, "He counteth all your sorrows," which introduces the chorus, "All ye that cried unto the Lord," which in turn leads into the famous duet and chorus, "I waited for the Lord."

Here at the end of the fifth number, or exactly halfway through the cantata, we reach the first pause, a pause which is in no sense a break or intermission, merely a preparing for the build-up of a magnificent climax. The sixth number is the aria, "The sorrows of death," still sung frequently in all churches where the tenor soloist is adequate, and in quite a number where he is not. This aria has everything a tenor likes, warm lyrical passages, dramatic climaxes on high notes, impressive pauses. The second half, beginning "We called through the darkness, Watchman, will the night soon pass?" is so fine that we marvel how the composer only a short while before could have written the solos in *St. Paul*.

The end of this admirable number is usually spoiled in a church performance, where it is presented by itself, and the tenor is allowed to sing the concluding phrase. The intended effect is quite different. In the cantata the tenor finishes with the question, "Will the night soon pass?" and after a pause, which should be almost painfully long, the solo soprano answers in the concluding phrase, "The night is departing." The unexpected change of voice startles, and the phrase seems far more triumphant than when it is sung by the tenor.

The words and notes of this concluding phrase become the theme of the following chorus, at the end of which there is a dramatic silence, and immediately the chorale, "Nun danket alle Gott," is sung, unaccompanied in the first stanza, with a flowing orchestral theme in the second. To remain on the pitch during the unaccompanied stanza puts any choir to the test. If the voices sag ever so little, the orchestra on its entrance shows them up painfully. Mendelssohn increased the difficulty by dividing the altos and the tenors, in the first stanza, and for one brief measure making the basses sing in octaves, so that the chorale is an exercise in six-part or even seven-part singing. Throughout the second stanza the chorus is in unison, until the last line, where the voices break into four parts.

Having composed the cantata so far as a practically uninterrupted unit, Mendelssohn now contrives a contrast, an interlude between all that has gone before and the final chorus. The ninth number is the beautiful duet for soprano and tenor, "My song shall be always Thy mercy," a completely successful escape from the duet-thirds in *St. Paul*. Number ten, "Ye nations offer to the Lord," the concluding chorus, is a succession of contrasts between contrapuntal and massive chord effects. The concluding phrase returns to the theme of the fugue in the first number of the cantata, "All that has life and breath, sing to the Lord."

The Hymn of Praise is probably best known for the duet and chorus, "I waited for the Lord," a kind of writing which characteristically appears in all Mendelssohn's oratorios. In the *St. Paul* its parallel is the chorus, "Happy and blest are they," in the *Elijah* it is the double chorus for women's voices, "He shall give His angels charge." In each instance the theme flows swiftly, yet is serene, and the simple melody haunts with a persistence difficult to explain. In such choral writing we are face to face again, as in the Songs Without Words, with Mendelssohn's gift for pure melody. The theme is as obvious as a folk tune, yet it is in some respects sophisticated. Hasty criticism may pronounce it trivial or banal, but this music once heard refuses to be dismissed. Other parts of a Mendelssohn oratorio we may outgrow, but at least one chorus, fast moving and serene, we always remember.

CHAPTER ELEVEN

Berlin

DURING HIS LEIPZIG PERIOD, IN THE
busy early years, Mendelssohn made two
more visits to England, the first in the
autumn of 1837, for several performances of *St. Paul,* the second in the
autumn of 1840, for the performance of
the *Hymn of Praise* at Birmingham.
On both visits, especially the first, he
made several appearances as organist
and as pianist, and the enthusiasm of the

123

audiences told him that his popularity with the English was still mounting. They liked the Gutenberg cantata but they also received the first oratorio with little adverse comment. If *St. Paul* survives today it is perhaps because the English keep it alive.

Then as now the English excelled in choral singing, and Mendelssohn, listening to magnificent renderings of his own msuic, was moved to equally magnificent praise. He wrote to the Sacred Harmonic Society, after their performance of *St. Paul,* that he could hardly express his gratification, that indeed he could never hear some parts of the work better executed. "The power of the choruses, this large body of good and musical voices and the style in which they sang my music, gave me the highest and most heartfelt pleasure. I could not but think of the inspiring influence which such a number of real amateurs must necessarily exercise on their fortunate country."

He returned to Leipzig with renewed energy and with fresh plans, not realizing that the large reputation which he was accumulating both at home and abroad would soon complicate his life and, through overwork, end it.

On June 7, 1840, there was a new King of Prussia, Frederick William IV, a music lover who admired Mendelssohn and at once determined to move him back from Leipzig to Berlin. His plan was to organize an Academy of Arts in four sections, devoted to painting, sculpture, architecture, and music, and to appoint Mendelssohn director of the music section. The offer was made officially

December 14, 1840, on terms which no doubt the King thought more than adequate. The salary was to be three thousand *thalers,* or about twenty-two hundred dollars, for which Mendelssohn was to assume the oversight of all the musical organizations already existing in Berlin, with a possible Conservatory, and from time to time take charge of certain concerts by the Royal Orchestra and singers from the Opera. The proposal was flattering but vague. The King, however well disposed to music, hadn't the slightest idea how Mendelssohn was to organize the Berlin musicians into a co-operating body, and Mendelssohn had excellent reasons for suspecting the thing couldn't be done. The King wanted merely to make of him a government official; he was determined to remain an artist.

His letters to his brother Paul state all the difficulties. To begin with, he doubted that Berlin could ever be a soil where a true musician, in spite of honors and money, would feel at home. The old *Singakademie* wound, which perhaps the King thought to heal, was still open. In the second place, the offer was not definite either as to what Mendelssohn was expected to accomplish or as to the authority which he could exercise. Was he merely to conduct the Royal Orchestra on certain occasions, or might he train the players, engage better where needed, and fix a regular schedule of rehearsals as well as of performances? No satisfactory reply came from the Prussian Court, perhaps because the King, ignorant of the subject into which his good intentions had plunged him, thought

Mendelssohn was displaying the crotchets of the musical temperament.

As to the proposed Conservatory, the King and his ministers instituted a few courses by way of a start, during the months they were negotiating with Mendelssohn, and it was evident that whatever they had in mind they were not thinking of a professional music school nor planning for the practical advancement of the art. Some of the courses in the composition department stirred Mendelssohn to bitter sarcasm, especially a series of lectures on The Relation of Music to the Plastic Arts and to the Stage, and another series described as A Guide to the Spiritual and the Worldly Drama.

At this very moment, when the King of Prussia was approaching Mendelssohn in the wrong way, the King of Saxony aroused himself to make the Leipzig Conservatory a reality. It is hard to understand why Mendelssohn wasted any more time over the Berlin proposals; the reason usually given, that he yielded to his mother's wish to have him near her, is not entirely convincing. He did at last give in, however, against his better judgment, and to his subsequent regret. The official report to the King and Mendelssohn's draft of a plan for the new Academy, are both revealing documents, one showing an artist's reluctance to do the wrong thing, the other suggesting an attempt to make the best of the situation by the enunciation of lofty ideals.

The Home Minister reported to the King on May 20, 1841:

"Your Majesty was pleased verbally to desire me to enter into communication with Herr Felix Mendelssohn-Bartholdy, in Leipzig, with a view to summon him to Berlin, and to fix his residence there by appointment. I therefore on the 11th of December last wrote to Herr Mendelssohn, in accordance with your Majesty's commands, and made the following offer:

"That he should be appointed Director of the musical class of the Academy of Arts, with a salary of three thousand thalers.

"I also mentioned that it was your Majesty's intention to reorganize the musical class of the Academy, and to connect it with some existing establishments for the development of musical cultivation, as well as with others yet to be formed; that Herr Mendelssohn's advice on the subject was requested; that he was to be appointed the future head of this institute. Further, that it was your Majesty's pleasure a certain number of concerts (to be hereafter fixed) were to be given every year under his direction, with the aid of the Royal orchestra and the members of the opera, in which oratorios especially, but also other works, such as symphonies, etc., were to be performed. Herr Mendelssohn, in two letters addressed to me, on the 15th December and the 2nd January, expressed his gratitude to your Majesty for so honorable an offer, as well as his entire satisfaction with regard to the title and the salary; he however reserved his full acceptance of the proposal until the duties involved in the situation offered to him in Berlin were more minutely detailed. The consci-

entiousness thus shown by Herr Mendelssohn cannot fail
to be acknowledged and respected; at the same time, he
promised to come to Berlin this spring.

"The Academy of Arts being regulated by the Ministerium of the departments of science, instruction, and
medicine, it was from this source alone that the wished-
for copy of the rules could be obtained for Herr Mendelssohn; as this, however, could not be immediately effected,
Minister Eichhorn resolved to discuss the whole affair
himself with Herr Mendelssohn regarding the reorganization of the musical class, and your Majesty was pleased
to permit the affair to rest for the time. Herr Mendelssohn,
according to his promise, recently came here, and he
adheres to his resolution not to accept any fixed situation
in your Majesty's service till he is previously informed
what duties he is expected to undertake.

"The proposed reforms in the musical section, which
are probably to be effected, in connection with many other
changes in the Academy of Arts, necessitate the dissolu-
tion of existing arrangements, and the formation of entirely new relations. The Royal Ministerium, if a larger
musical institute were established, would put in their
claim for the Royal Theatre, which, by previous regula-
tions of existing institutes, must be included, along with
most of the artists attached to it. The sum of money
requisite for this purpose must be fixed and granted.
These are all reasons which prevent the Royal Ministerium, within so short a period, being able to arrange
such a comprehensive affair sufficiently to lay these pro-

posals before your Majesty, and also render it impossible to define the situation for Herr Mendelssohn, or to prescribe the duties which, as Director of the musical class, he must undertake to fulfill.

"Herr Mendelssohn, on the other hand, must declare, in the course of a few weeks, whether it is his intention to give up his situation in Leipzig or not: he therefore presses for a decision.

"Under these circumstances, with the express stipulation, however, of your Majesty's approbation, I have made the following proposal to Herr Mendelssohn:

"That for the present he should only for a certain period fix his residence in Berlin—say, a year—placing himself at your Majesty's disposal, in return for which, your Majesty should confer on him the title of Capellmeister, but without imposing on him the performance of the duties of this office in the Royal Opera; likewise the previously named salary of three thousand thalers pro anno to be bestowed on him; during this time, however, he is neither to hold any office, nor to undertake any definite duties, unless in the course of this period Herr Eichhorn should furnish him with the long wished-for details, and he should declare himself satisfied with them, in which case the reserved consent as to a definitive nomination should ensue.

"Herr Mendelssohn has already assured me that he is prepared to accept the proposal, and if your Majesty be pleased to give your consent, Herr Eichhorn would gain time to consult with Herr Mendelssohn on this affair, and to place distinct proposals before your Majesty. From the well known honorable character of Herr Mendelssohn, it may be confidently anticipated that in this kind of interim relation he will be the more anxious to devote all his powers to your Majesty, from the very fact of his duties not being more closely defined. Such a relation, however, can only be advisable for a certain time; one year has therefore been agreed on. If, contrary to expectation, the reorganization of the musical class of the Academy and the establishment of a musical institute be not so carried out as to cause Herr Mendelssohn the conviction of finding a field of activity for his bent and his vocation, or if the claims on him should prevent his acceptance, or, lastly—which I subjoin at the express desire of Herr Mendelssohn—should the expectations now entertained by your Majesty with regard to him not be fulfilled, then the relation now formed shall be dissolved at the end of the appointed period on the above conditions, and, therefore, in an honorable manner.

"Herr Eichhorn, whom I have informed of the proposal made through me to Herr Mendelssohn, and also of his acceptance, has, on his side, stated no objections.

"Your Majesty's decision is respectfully solicited at your pleasure; and, awaiting your Majesty's further commands, I am, with the deepest reverence,

"Your Majesty's faithful servant,

V. Massow."

Mendelssohn's plan for the Academy is not dated, but it obviously was written for the royal eyes.

"It is proposed to establish a German Music Academy in Berlin, to concentrate in one common focus the now isolated efforts in the sphere of instruction in art, in order to guide rising artists in a solid and earnest direction, thus· imparting to the musical sense of the nation a new and more energetic impetus; for this purpose, on one side, the already existing institutes and their members must be concentrated, and on the other, the aid of new ones must be called in.

"Among the former may be reckoned the various Royal Academies for musical instruction, which must be united with this Musical Academy, and carried on as branches of the same, with greater or less modifications, in one sense and in one direction. In these are included, for example, the Institute for Éléves of the Royal Orchestra; the Organ Institute; that of the Theatre (limited to the theatre alone) for instruction in singing, declamation, etc. Further, the members of the Royal Capelle must be required to give instruction on their various instruments. A suitable locality can no doubt be found among the royal buildings, and also a library, with the requisite old and new musical works, scores, and books.

"The new appointments to consist of—

"1. A head teacher of composition; the best that can be found in Germany, to give regular instructions in theory, thorough-bass, counterpoint, and fugues.

"2. A head teacher of solo singing; also the best to be had in Germany.

"3. A head teacher of choral singing, who should strive

to acquire personal influence over the scholars under his
care, by good pianoforte playing and steady direction.

"4. A head teacher of pianoforte playing, for which
office a man of the most unquestionable talent and reputation must alone be selected. The other teachers for these
departments could be found in Berlin itself; nor would
there be any difficulty in procuring teachers of aesthetics,
the history of music, etc.

"The complete course to last three years; the scholars,
after previous examination, to be instructed gratis; no
prize works to be admitted but at stated periods; all the
works of the scholars, from the time of their admission,
to be collected and criticized in connection with each
other, and subsequently a prize (probably consisting of
a sum sufficient for a long journey through Germany,
Italy, France, and England) to be adjudged accordingly.
Every winter a certain number of concerts to take place,
in which all the teachers (including the above-named
members of the Royal Capelle) must cooperate, and by
which, through the selection of the music, as well as by its
execution, direct influence may be gained over the ma-
jority of the public.

"The following principle must serve as a basis for the
whole Institute: that every sphere of art can only elevate
itself above a mere handicraft by being devoted to the
expression of lofty thought, along with the utmost possible technical finish, and a pure and intellectual aim;
that also solidity, precision, and strict discipline in teaching and learning should be considered the first law, thus

not falling short in this respect of any handicraft; that in every department, all teaching and learning should be exclusively devoted to the thoughts intended to be expressed, and to that more elevated mood, to which technical perfection in art must ever be subordinate."

While the negotiations were proceeding with Berlin, Mendelssohn's Leipzig friends were not a little shocked and grieved by the discovery that he would leave them. The letters of his sisters and his mother show how strong the pressure was from the family to come where they might all be reunited, yet it remains a puzzle why Mendelssohn imperiled his great work at the Gewandhaus and his plans for the Leipzig Conservatory, knowing as he did that his chance for happiness in Berlin was slight. As we have seen from the report to the King, he committed himself only to a single experimental year, but the experiment continued with less and less satisfaction to himself for the short remainder of his days. It would not be over-fantastic to say that the Berlin engagement killed him. He became the victim of a tug of war between the King of Saxony and the King of Prussia, each trying to make his chief city attractive to Mendelssohn, and each furnishing him with more opportunities for work than one man could undertake. The ensuing years were divided between Leipzig and Berlin with frequent and busy visits to England, constant appearances at various festivals in Germany, and an altogether incredible amount of teaching and composing. Was Felix Mendelssohn such a happy man as legend has made him? Before he came to the end, the score for him, as for other human beings, was fairly balanced.

His Leipzig chapter closed on Palm Sunday, April 4, 1841, when he performed the *St. Matthew Passion* in St. Thomas's Church. By early autumn he was installed in Berlin in a house opposite his old family home, furiously busy composing for the *Antigone* of Sophocles, which the King of Prussia wished performed. The play was given at Potsdam on October 28, and the success of the noble story, enriched by Mendelssohn's music, was repeated in many performances elsewhere. On January 10, 1842, *St. Paul* was given at the King's command, and had very slight success indeed. Without difficulty we can now explain its cold reception in Berlin by its own essential defects, but Mendelssohn felt that the orchestra was hostile and the audience unfriendly. They may have been. We remember, however, that he was already a tired man, making inhuman drains on his nervous system. Having completed his "Scotch" Symphony, he made a flying trip to Leipzig in March to produce it. In May he was at Düsseldorf, conducting the Lower Rhine Festival for the sixth time. In June and July he took his wife and his "Scotch" Symphony to England for what was to be a vacation, but it turned out to be perhaps the busiest of his visits. In August he and his wife joined his brother Paul in Switzerland for a true vacation at last. His thoughts began to occupy themselves with the past. From Interlaken he wrote his mother, recalling that twenty years before, in his boyhood, the family had stopped there, in a charming little inn shaded by large walnut trees. The landlady, then good looking and young, had made an impression upon him. Ten years later he had stopped again on a walking tour, so shabby and dust-covered that the same landlady would not give him a room—not at least, as we may suppose, until he paid in advance. Now, he writes, he is back in the same place, once more accepted as a solid member of society.

Artist that he was, it had become his ironic fate to have dealings, not altogether happy, with kings. From the English visit, however, he brought away delightful mem-ories of the young Queen Victoria and the Prince Con-sort. His letter to his mother, July 19, tells of Prince Albert's invitation to Buckingham Palace to try the organ, and of the charming minutes he spent with the most human of royal lovers.

"I found him alone, and as we were talking away, the Queen came in, also alone, in a simple morning dress. . . . Then Prince Albert proceeded to explain the stops to me, and she said that she would meanwhile put things straight. I begged that the Prince would first play me something, so that, as I said, I might boast about it in Germany; and he played a Choral, by heart, with the pedals, so charmingly and clearly and correctly that it would have done credit to any professional, and the Queen, having finished her work, came and sat by him and listened and looked pleased. Then it was my turn, and I began my chorus from 'St. Paul'—'How lovely are the messengers.' Before I got to the end of the first

verse they both joined in the chorus, and all the time
Prince Albert managed the stops for me so cleverly—
first a flute, at the *forte* the great organ, at the D major
part the whole register, then he made a lovely diminuendo
with the stops, and so on to the end of the piece, and all
by heart—till I was really quite enchanted. Then the
young Prince of Gotha came in and there was more chat-
ting; and the Queen asked if I had written any new songs,
and said she was very fond of singing my published ones.
'You should sing one to him,' said Prince Albert; and
after a little begging, she said she would try the 'Früh-
lings-lied' in B flat—'if it is still here,' she added, 'for
all my music is packed up for Claremont.' Prince Albert
went to look for it, but came back, saying it was already
packed. 'But one might perhaps unpack it,' said I. 'We
must send for Lady ——,' she said (I did not catch the
name). So the bell was rung and the servants were sent
after it, but without success; and at last the Queen went
herself, and while she was gone Prince Albert said to me,
'She begs you will accept this present as a remembrance,'
and gave me a little case with a beautiful ring, on which
is engraved 'V.R. 1842.' Then the Queen came back and
said, 'Lady —— is gone, and has taken all my things
with her. It really is most annoying.' (You can't think
how that amused me.) I then begged that I might not be
made to suffer for the accident, and hoped she would
sing another song. After some consultation with her
husband he said, 'She will sing you something of
Gluck's.' Meantime the Princess of Gotha had come in,

and we five proceeded through various corridors and rooms to the Queen's sitting-room, where there was a gigantic rocking-horse standing near the sofa, and two big bird-cages, and pictures on the walls, and splendidly bound books on the table, and music on the piano. The Duchess of Kent came in too, and while they were all talking I rummaged about amongst the music, and soon discovered my first set of songs. So, of course, I begged her rather to sing one of those than the Gluck, to which she very kindly consented; and which did she choose?— 'Schöner und schöner schmückt sich!' sung it quite charmingly in strict time and tune, and with very good execution. Only in the line 'Der Prosa Lasten und Müh,' where it goes down to D, and then comes up again by semi-tones, she sang D sharp each time, and as I gave her the note the two first times, the last time she sang D, where it ought to have been D sharp. But with the exception of this little mistake it was really charming, and the last long G I have never heard better, or purer, or more natural from any amateur. Then I was obliged to confess that Fanny had written the song (which I found very hard, but pride must have a fall), and beg her to sing one of my own also. If I would give her plenty of help she would gladly try, she said, and then she sang the Pilgerspruch, 'Lass dich nur,' really quite faultlessly, and with charming feeling and expression. I thought to myself, one must not pay too many compliments on such an occasion, so I merely thanked her a great many times; upon which she said, 'Oh, if only I had not been so frightened; generally I have such long breath.' Then I praised her heartily and with the best conscience in the world; for just that part with the long C at the close she had done so well, taking it and the three notes next to it all in the same breath, as one seldom hears it done—and therefore it amused me doubly that she herself should have begun about it. After this Prince Albert sang the Erndte-lied, 'Es ist ein Schnitter'; and then he said I must play him something before I went, and gave me as themes the Choral which he had played on the organ and the song he had just sung. If everything had gone as usual, I ought to have improvised dreadfully badly, for it is almost always so with me when I want it to go well, and then I should have gone away vexed with the whole morning. But just as if I were to keep nothing but the pleasantest, most charming recollection of it, I never improvised better."

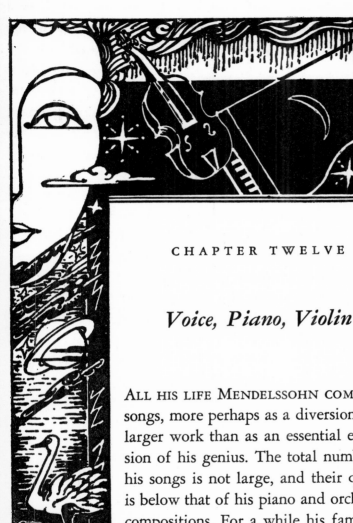

CHAPTER TWELVE

Voice, Piano, Violin

ALL HIS LIFE MENDELSSOHN COMPOSED
songs, more perhaps as a diversion from
larger work than as an essential expression of his genius. The total number of
his songs is not large, and their quality
is below that of his piano and orchestral
compositions. For a while his fame carried them, but even by amateurs they
are now seldom performed except in
England.

He loved great poetry; if his taste had not been fastidious, he might have been satisfied more easily with available texts for an opera. We are not surprised that for his songs he chose fine verses. As we said on an earlier page, some peculiarity in his talent made it hard for him to set words to music. The spirit of a poem he could translate so long as the words were suppressed, but to join the text to an adequate melody was in most cases beyond him.

This is all the more strange because he had Schubert for an immediate predecessor, and Robert Schumann for contemporary and companion. The art of great song-writing flourished in Germany during the nineteenth century, yet he added nothing to it, and was hardly in the stream. His songs are best when they are least ambitious, when they pretend to be nothing more than folk tunes. Even in his more elaborate songs there is repetition rather than development, and whatever ambition there is, shows only in the accompaniment. A song with words, a song for the human voice, seems to have been for Mendelssohn a singable phrase or two, charming enough to be heard two or three times.

We remember that the songs of Robert Burns were written for just such folk tunes, repeated with each stanza, and Mendelssohn knew well how difficult it was to compose a strain of unadorned beauty. He was a great admirer of folk song in his own country and in Great Britain; why shouldn't he try to reproduce in sophisticated art the folk manner? No reason at all, but unfortunately he didn't succeed. In many of his songs he achieves the bareness of a folk tune but only on occasion the authentic and haunting beauty.

Most lovers of Mendelssohn will offer exceptions to this verdict, and a few enthusiasts will reject it entirely. If we were gathered around the piano, however, with the collected songs before us, we'd probably agree that the ones we like have at some time or other made appeal because we heard them well sung. The luck of all of us has not been the same. If the song you favor is one which I've heard badly sung, my opinion of it will be low. Bad singers find little to discourage them in Mendelssohn's songs. His comment on Queen Victoria's skill in rendering "Lass dich nur" is no more than a compliment on her ability to hold a fairly low note through several measures. It is fair to say in general that the songs ask technical skill of only the most modest kind, but the singer can put into the music a beauty that isn't there, or he can give merely a literal reading of the text. You may protest that any song into which beauty can be read is a good song. Into the best of Mendelssohn, however, or of any other great composer, the importation of quality does not need to be wholesale.

The songs, especially the part-songs, have suffered, as I said, because they are easy for poor singers to execute. In most cases they lend themselves to sentimental renderings, and the opportunity is rarely missed, yet even those who like myself are critical of them, have a few favorites. The Spring Song (Fruehlingslied), Opus 19, No. 1, composed in Mendelssohn's twenty-first year, is charming, full of musical phrases which later composers have echoed. The flow of the accompaniment and the serenity of the melody may or may not express for you the springtime which the words refer to, but the music as music is altogether lovely.

The student should compare the Venetianisches Gondellied, Opus 57, No. 5, with the Gondola pieces among the Songs Without Words. Mendelssohn catches the same romantic atmosphere, but the text by Thomas Moore was apparently no aid to inspiration. The student should also compare Felix Mendelssohn's songs with those by his sister Fanny, which he included in his collection. It may be argued that Fanny was the song writer of the family.

Next to the Spring Song I would choose the Volkslied, Opus 47, No. 4, composed in Leipzig in 1839. Here the simplicity of folk art is captured with success, and the theme is distinguished. I wish I could list also among my favorites Auf Flügeln des Gesanges, Opus 34, No. 2, the most often performed and the most overpraised of Mendelssohn's songs, but I fear the best thing about it is the Heine lyric to which the sweetish and banal melody is fitted.

Mendelssohn composed for the piano much that we now rate little higher than the songs, much that, like the songs, can be made to sound better than it really is, but he also produced more than one man's share of masterpieces, some of them dating curiously from the same month or week as his less lucky songs. Of the finest piano things, those still constantly played in addition to the Songs Without Words, are the Prelude and Fugue in E minor, the Rondo Capriccioso, the Variations Sérieuses, the Piano Concerto in G minor, and the Violin Concerto. The Prelude and Fugue in E minor was published as No. 1 of the Six Preludes and Six Fugues, Opus 35, the Prelude belonging to 1837, the year of publication, the Fugue having been composed earlier. In both Prelude and Fugue the influence of Sebastian Bach is clear, but the music is original, singularly vigorous, sturdy and modern, and altogether in the piano idiom. The emotional range of the piece, the mingling of lyrical and dramatic elements, is astonishing. The Prelude, passionate and stormy, contrasts with the quiet opening of the Fugue, and the mounting climax of the Fugue is capped by the majestic chorale at the end. Admirable as the Prelude is, the Fugue, composed when Mendelssohn was only seventeen, surprises us still by its noble seriousness, its almost tragic depth. According to Schubring's "Reminiscences," the Fugue was written by the death bed, or shortly after the death of a boyhood friend, and the chorale, closing the Fugue in the major key, was intended to express the comfort of eternal rest. Particularly fine are the last three measures with the gradual diminuendo and the soaring theme.

The Rondo Capriccioso is one of those lucky pieces beloved by amateurs as well as professionals, gnawed at by the beginner, transmuted into gossamer by the virtuoso, yet however played, fresh and spontaneous as the 'Midsummer Night' music. Indeed the Rondo was composed at almost the same time as the *Midsummer Night's Dream* Overture, and it has the same scherzo-like deftness. If it lacks the profundity which marks the E minor Fugue, it compensates by lyrical beauty and elfin gaiety.

The Variations Sérieuses were composed in 1841, just before Mendelssohn left Leipzig for Berlin. The art of writing variations on a theme had been carried to a classical perfection by Mozart and to extraordinary heights by Beethoven. Mendelssohn's contemporaries, Robert Schumann, for example, were developing the

form romantically, treating the theme freely and introducing effects which were little short of orchestral. It is
usually said that Mendelssohn in this magnificent composition returned to the classical model, varying the melodic
subject without pushing the changes beyond recognition,
and respecting throughout the piano idiom. But we call
some of the passages orchestral when we try to describe
the variations and contrasts of tone color, and others we
think of as organ-like. Here perhaps is the best corrective
to that incomplete understanding of Mendelssohn which
defines his genius as cheerful, graceful, sentimental, at
times a little obvious. This music is what he called it,
serious; in every phrase of it a profound nature is re-
vealed, a thoughtful nature, aware of tragedy.

The theme is interesting in two ways, which promise at
once two different developments in the series of variations. The melody is grave, yet it suggests strong emotion.
Indeed a discreet performer will be careful not to spend
all the passion at once, leaving nothing for the fuller state-
ments later. The melody implies also strong harmonic
modulations and developments, which are at once clearly
indicated but are only realized further on. Altogether the
effect of the theme is challenging, and the attention once
caught, is held firmly.

In the first variation the melody is repeated unchanged
with a running accompaniment in the right hand and
staccato octaves in the left. It has been said with justice
that there is nothing difficult about this variation except
that nobody but an artist can play it. It calls for a contrast

between the legato melody, the agitated accompaniment and the staccato bass, and the contrast is made by three distinct kinds of touch.

The second variation changes the melody and embroiders the harmonies, the right hand maintaining the melody while both hands care for an agitated accompaniment in two voices. The massive third variation, built out of staccato chords and octaves, gives us the first orchestral suggestion. By contrast the fourth variation is thoroughly pianistic, a treatment of the theme in a free canon, to be played staccato with extreme lightness. Very difficult, and very beautiful.

The fifth variation presents the theme approximately in the form in which we first heard it, the purpose being to fix it again in our mind before the variations become more complicated. No. 6, with its sharp contrasts of upper and lower registers, would not be so effective if we hadn't just heard No. 5. Variations 7, 8, and 9, each distinct but all accumulating toward a climax, follow approximately the harmonic sequences of the original theme, but are built chiefly on the first phrase of its melody. Out of the same phrase develops the quiet fugue of No. 10 and the song-like meditation of No. 11.

In the twelfth variation an orchestral effect is achieved by the sharply hammered broken chords, all by way of creating a lovely contrast in No. 13. Here the original melody is played with the thumb and first finger of the left hand, the other fingers supplying staccato bass notes, while the right hand is busy with a running figure, light and staccato. Variation 14, the *adagio,* serves as a moment of extreme quiet before the buildup of the finale. Throughout variation 15 the music becomes agitated, more so in 16, still more so throughout 17, until the final *presto* is reached.

If the Variations Sérieuses do not appear on current programs as often as they deserve it is probably because Brahms now gives the pianist a better chance to show his abilities, but if you have heard Paderewski play the Mendelssohn Variations, you have an insight into their importance.

The Piano Concerto in G minor, the one which is now most often performed, is a brilliant show-piece, far more obviously popular than the Variations Sérieuses, though musically not so profound. The first movement, *multo con fuoco,* calls for some first-rate octave playing and passage work. Occasional quiet intervals foretell the modulation into the *andante* in G major. The theme of the *andante* is what we call Mendelssohnian when we wish to describe a melodiousness which unless the player is on his guard will sound too sweet. The player must take even greater care with the *multo allegro* of the concluding movement, which starts off in a triumphant march, equally susceptible to distinguished interpretation or the opposite, and which quickly goes into a rapid pattern of broken chords, entrancingly effective if the notes are played with mathematical evenness. Such music was written expressly for one of Mendelssohn's styles of playing. His impeccable technique, the deftness and delicacy which were thought phenomenal in his time, elevated all such passages to unexpected importance. We should take care to remember that this, as we've just said, was only one of his styles of playing. His performance of the G major Concerto of Beethoven was thought supreme in his day and is still remembered in tradition. This G minor Concerto of his obviously made small demands on one part of his resources, and that the nobler part, yet when properly executed it is a lovely thing, likely to keep its place in the pianistic repertoire.

If the Piano Concerto must be praised in measured terms the Violin Concerto places no such obligation upon us. It still ranks with the very best in violin literature. Mendelssohn was himself an accomplished string player, and could doubtless have written an effective concerto without the aid of a virtuoso, but it is equally certain that his concerto profited from his friend David's criticism and advice. All violinists admire the idiomatic writing for their instrument, and all audiences succumb to the charm of the music, the song-like quality of the *andante,* the joyous brilliance of the concluding section. For pure content, for musical feeling and thoughtfulness, not even the Violin Concerto matches the Variations, but to make such distinctions between masterpieces seems ungracious, and few of us, immediately after hearing the Violin Concerto well played, would care to reckon it second to anything else.

CHAPTER THIRTEEN

The Larger Midsummer Night's Dream

AT THE END OF THE FIRST BERLIN YEAR
Mendelssohn realized that the plans for
an academy would fail. He had given
concerts and composed music, the King
of Prussia maintained his personal interest in his musical dreams for the city, but
there was something wrong; neither the
state authorities nor the musicians nor
the public made any great effort to bring
about in Berlin what Mendelssohn had

149

accomplished in Leipzig. The fault lay partly in himself. He adored Leipzig and he disliked Berlin. The amount of commuting he did between the two cities staggers us when we recall the slowness of travel in those days, and the Berliners can hardly be blamed if they thought his heart was elsewhere. No progress was made toward a building for the music school of the academy, the Royal orchestra remained as it was, fair but sadly below the Gewandhaus standard, and though Mendelssohn at the King's request composed incidental music for special plays and sacred music for important ceremonies, he had no real authority in either the theatre or the churches, and since the decline of the *Singakademie* there was no choral group of the first rank.

Why did he stay beyond this disappointing year? The question has never been answered. It is true that his mother was in poor health and that the family bond among the Mendelssohns was always strong, but the constant absences from Berlin take from the force of this reason. It may be true, as some biographers have urged, that for the family's sake as well as for his own he did not wish to leave Berlin a second time under a cloud of something like defeat. The *Singakademie* election, according to this theory, still rankled. But if his motive in staying was to gain a great Berlin success, why didn't he concentrate on that one purpose?

Fearing that he might leave, the King of Prussia promised at least to form a small chorus of excellent singers and a small but virtuoso orchestra to give music of Men-

delssohn's choice or composition. Was the King too thinking of the *Singakademie* affair, and therefore furnishing
the equipment for Mendelssohn to show what he would
have done had he been elected conductor? It would have
been childish for Mendelssohn to set any value on such
revenge. Yet he stayed in Berlin indefinitely, first asking
that his salary be reduced and that he be permitted still
greater freedom of travel, and later retiring from most of
his remaining responsibilities. For the time being he accepted the title of General Music Director, his duties consisting chiefly of the supervision of church music and the
composition of embellishments to the famous plays which
the King of Prussia might wish to revive.

Simultaneously, as though to keep him in a state of in-
decision, the King of Saxony took definite steps to endow
the Leipzig Conservatory. Since this institution was Mendelssohn's favorite project, there was never any serious
doubt that he would give his time to it as soon as it was
established. His mother died suddenly in December, 1842,
but even if she had lived beyond the opening of the Conservatory in the spring of the following year, Leipzig
would undoubtedly have claimed most of his attention.

The explanation of his strange reluctance to sever himself entirely from Berlin lay probably in a personal trait
which though natural and creditable enough is usually
passed over in silence by his biographers. From those
early days when he conducted the Sunday concerts in his
father's house he was a performer, endowed heavily with
that histrionic temperament which craves an audience, as

many different audiences as possible. In this he resembled Liszt rather than his idol Bach. He was a concertizing artist. It was altogether for the benefit of music that he should be so, and we take with a grain of salt his frequently expressed wish that he might settle down in one place. The wish was a human one and he believed it sincere, but his temperament refused to let him take root in Düsseldorf or England or Leipzig or Berlin. Equally his temperament forbade him to decline invitations to those or any other places. He would have come to the United States if time and strength had been more plentiful.

But he hadn't the strength even for what he tried to do, and the combination of Leipzig and Berlin, with continued visits to Great Britain, brought him to an early grave. His schedule would have been possible had he been only a virtuoso performer, or only a conductor, or only one of the most prolific composers, or only an imaginative and conscientious pioneer in musical education, but he led all these careers simultaneously, and when it became obvious that he must break under the strain, he was unable to give up any of them. For his own good he should have discontinued the trips to England, which used up his energy, but the English audience was in some respects his most precious; his friends across the Channel had acclaimed him in his youth and had remained more than faithful. He might have said no to the Lower Rhine Festival and to the other German festivals which since his Düsseldorf days had called upon him almost every year. He might have taken his farewell of Berlin, but the King of Prussia was after all a friendly and well-meaning patron, and through him there could be found, if not a conservatory to equal what the King of Saxony would establish, at least certain scattered opportunities which a composer would be glad of.

For example, the opportunity which came in July, 1843. Mendelssohn's success in furnishing incidental music for certain Greek tragedies roused the King of Prussia to put on a Shakespearian play, and after consultation with his General Music Director he chose the *Midsummer Night's Dream*. We are not surprised. All his life Mendelssohn had loved Shakespeare's fairy masque, the Overture written in his youth had been his first and greatest song without words, and the opportunity to set the entire text to music, or the best moments of it, for actual presentation on the stage, must have revived his long-discouraged wish to compose an opera.

Midsummer Night's Dream, as he now treated it in full, is of course not changed into an opera, and the enlarged score furnishes ample proof, if proof were needed, that his genius was for the concert stage rather than for the theatre. The "Dream" music is a symphonic suite, an interpretive supplement to the play rather than a setting of it. Two numbers have exceeded in popularity the famous Overture—the magical Scherzo and the exuberant Wedding March, to the sound of which a formidable parade of just-married Anglo-Saxons have walked out of church. In fact it is now difficult to imagine a conventional wedding among English-speaking people before Wagner composed *Lohengrin* and Mendelssohn completed the music for *Midsummer Night's Dream.*

Rarely do composers or indeed creative artists of any kind succeed in a belated return to an early inspiration. Either the flame has burned low or maturing years have changed its quality. The difference between the first and the second parts of Goethe's *Faust,* to cite a notable example, is a hurdle too bold for most readers. Mendelssohn, however, was able to go on exactly from where he left off. The enlarged treatment of the "Dream" continues the mood of the youthful Overture as though the whole were planned and finished at the same time.

Here is an invitation for speculation which biographers and critics have not declined. Does the unity of the later with the earlier music signify that Mendelssohn's faculties remained static? Or was his control over various moods so exceptional that he could write at any time in any vein, as a versatile actor can assume any role? These questions have been asked, but the answer to neither of them, if we had it, would be illuminating. The music would remain inimitable and like all beautiful things unexplained. When we remember that Mendelssohn composed it in a year of sorrow and worry and failing health, we recognize with wonder and awe the authentic spark from heaven. His faculties certainly did not remain static; he was shortly to give us, in the *Elijah,* a startling example of self-development in a field where he had shown no precocious talent. But if the theme of the Shakespearian play inspired the same happy result at two distinct periods of his life, the reason may profitably be sought, to some extent, in the theme rather than exclusively in Mendelssohn.

Midsummer Night's Dream, as all the world knows, is a fanciful mixture of the fairyland over which Oberon and Titania preside and the humdrum world in which Bottom and Quince and the other well-meaning thickheads earn their living as weaver, tailor, tinker, and ordinarily keep clear of poetry. But now Theseus their Prince is to marry Hippolyta, and the clowns determine to offer an amateur play for the entertainment of the bride and bridegroom. The subject of their play is the tragic death of Pyramus and Thisbe. They rehearse the ridiculous script after working hours, in the forest, on Midsummer Night, and become involved with the love affairs of Lysander and Hermia and of Demetrius and Helena, mortal lovers— also with the love quarrel of the King and Queen of fairyland. Oberon sends Puck to put an enchantment upon Titania, and the sprite while he has his hand in puts an ass's head on Bottom and confuses the human quartet. Since Theseus and Hippolyta are in the background and Pyramus and Thisbe are in the wedding entertainment, each group of characters illustrates some kind of love, or various degrees of madness in love. Shakespeare states the theme on which he is playing variations:

> *"The lunatic, the lover and the poet*
> *Are of imagination all compact."*

155

That Mendelssohn was interested greatly or permanently in the mad things men and women will do when in love, there is no reason to believe, but the mystery of the imagination always fascinated him, as it must every creative artist. In his youth he had encountered early that kind of common sense which has no imagination at all; in his last years he was still colliding with Bottoms and Quinces in the realm of officialdom, among educators, most painful of all, among colleagues who thought themselves artists. Shakespeare had satirized the stupid in the only way which would not be too cruel; he had laughed at them, but he had blunted your scorn by making you think. Very casually he had asked whether reality is in the senses or in the mind, whether Bottom and his crew, lacking imagination, understand the world they live in, whether we mortals can ever take possession of our world at all until we look for it in the mind and the heart.

Shakespeare provokes our thought about imaginative art, perhaps lets us overhear his own ideas, in the comments of Theseus and Hippolyta on Bottom's theatrical entertainment, as it is at last performed. The clowns could understand everything about the theatre except what makes a play possible, the dramatic conventions. You must have at least enough imagination to concede a three-sided room; if you insist on the fourth wall between you and the actors, you'll miss the show. Though six people are on the stage, only one must speak at a time, or you'll miss the dialogue. Art is practicable only for those who can make believe—and perhaps only for the same imaginative folk is life livable. The ability to make believe must be in the audience as well as in the artist; the artist is not so rare, alas, as the imaginative listener.

Bottom and his fellows reason soundly, their logic is perfect, their intentions are excellent, they show respect for culture by attempting to stage an old story, one of the most famous in the world, but they seem complete fools because they are devoid of imagination. They have none themselves, they don't miss it, they don't expect it in others. The script of their play calls for a roaring lion, and only with reluctance do they tolerate a roar by one of their number, since the real thing can't be had. But suppose someone in the audience should think the roaring genuine and take fright? Against this awkward possibility they introduce a prologue to explain that the lion is make-believe and there's no danger. So moonlight is represented by one with a lantern, and another prologue explains that the lantern isn't the real moon.

Is the nonsense carried too far? Hippolyta thinks it is. After a few minutes of inadequate scenery and literal-minded explanations, she says that this is the silliest stuff she ever heard. Theseus gives a profound answer:

"The best in this kind are but shadows,
And the worst are no worse, if imagination mend them."

To which Hippolyta replies justly:

"It must be your imagination then, and not theirs."

157

Mendelssohn knew the play by heart, not only the passages of exquisite fancy but the lines of searching truth. Shakespeare could lay a finger on the heart of experience even in his lighter moods. Must we always be solemn in order to be profound? Must we take our philosophy in three dimensions and by weight, as Wagner dispenses it? I prefer the *Midsummer Night's Dream,* and Shakespeare and Mendelssohn. The ideas in the play, though merely touched on, will last any man a lifetime.

It is said that the contrasting groups of characters, the fairies, the human lovers, the clowns, are clearly indicated in the Overture. The whole suite shows the groups more clearly differentiated. The Overture stands as Mendelssohn had originally composed it. The first number thereafter is the Scherzo, to be played at the end of Act One. We are left in no doubt as to which group of characters the Scherzo represents; even if the music itself does not tell us, we get an unmistakable hint from the use of its themes to accompany the dialogue of Puck and the fairies, and to build up the music for the entrance of Oberon and his train, and for the appearance, on the other side of the stage, of Titania, his estranged Queen. This fairy music, the second number of the suite, though it trails suggestions of the Scherzo, reminds us also of the Overture, a little as though we were listening once more to a theme with variations. The third number is a song with chorus, a setting of the words which Titania asks her attendants to sing, "You spotted snakes with double tongues," less often heard than the purely orchestral sections. I am in

158

danger of pressing an idea too far, yet I venture to repeat that Mendelssohn interprets a text most successfully when he doesn't use the words. In the *Elijah* he refutes this criticism, but not I think in the chorus of *Midsummer Night's Dream*.

In the fourth number the human lovers are introduced, the music accompanying the dialogue between Puck and Oberon as Lysander and Hermia enter, and after them Demetrius and Helena. The fifth number, to be played at the end of Act Two, is a passionate allegro describing the happy state of the young people before Puck has tricked their eyes and tangled their loyalties. With a sudden speeding of the tempo the music turns humorous, introducing Bottom, Quince, Flute, Snout and their company. The sixth number accompanies the rehearsal of the Pyramus and Thisbe play, incidental music which merely points the comedy until Titania appears, bewitched, and Bottom, her new admiration, wearing the ass's head.

The seventh number describes the reconciliation of the human lovers after Puck's mischief is remedied, the eighth number portrays the reconciliation of Oberon and Titania, and the ninth is the Wedding March for Theseus and Hippolyta. Happy as these three numbers are, they are naturally of a deeper character than the comic sections, more poetic, in a way more serious.

The tenth number contains the accompaniment for the Pyramus play, measures extremely witty and all too brief. Few things in music are so downright funny as the tenth number, the funeral march for the unfortunate Pyramus, scored for clarinet, bassoon and drum. The eleventh number is a dance for the clowns. The twelfth number, the finale, begins with a repetition of the Wedding March, then returns to the themes of the Overture.

These numbers are quite obviously grouped around the classes of character in the play—the fairies, the most imaginative; the human lovers, who occupy middle ground; the company of clowns, who have common sense but no imagination at all. Taken together they constitute the population, not of the fabulous Athenian wood, but of the world as Shakespeare found it—and you and I—and Felix Mendelssohn.

Skilful pianists have arranged the Scherzo for their instrument, and we all have heard the Wedding March on the organ, but we shan't know the *Midsummer Night's Dream* music until we hear it played by the orchestra. Like all Mendelssohn's important work, it is available on phonograph records, and there's no excuse for studying it except as he wished us to hear it. His skill in scoring for the orchestra, his uncanny instinct for the perfect combination to convey his meaning, may have been the result of his childhood opportunities to experiment with an orchestra in his father's house.

Or it may have been something inevitable in his character, which would have matured in him even though his opportunities had been fewer.

CHAPTER FOURTEEN

Elijah

THE IDEA OF A DRAMATIC ORATORIO ON the story of Elijah had engaged Mendelssohn for several years, but he seems to have concentrated seriously on the work only when his health was failing. That he believed he was near the end of his life we cannot surely say, yet the feverish intensity with which he completed his masterpiece suggests that he was not without a premonition.

Though the family letters continue to furnish a detailed picture of these closing years, they do not tell us as much as we could wish of his inner life. The record of his heart is in his music. In certain obvious ways he must have been a happy man; he continued to enjoy success as an artist, his Conservatory attracted from the first pupils of great talent, his family life was serene, undisturbed by any trouble except the usual sicknesses of children and the natural sorrows of time, as his elders aged and died. He had never to worry about money. He was singularly free to give all his strength to his work. Yet these rare blessings to a man of his conscience were heavy responsibilities. More nearly perhaps than other geniuses he made the most of his talents, and whether he was satisfied with the result we may well doubt. Without being oversubtle in our conjectures we are tempted to believe that in spite of his prodigious activities and his innumerable friendships he was at the end a lonely man.

For one thing, he had begun his career with more than the optimism of youth. The personal success to which he justifiably looked forward was almost immediately realized, but even in his youngest days he was no egoist; he had dreamt of a new era for music in his country, a raising of standards, a revival of the national tradition in German music, to which he hoped to contribute, but which would progress beyond him. In spite of the healthy promise in the Leipzig conservatory and the superb achievements at the Gewandhaus he had learned that popular taste is hard to mold and harder still to make permanent, and that prejudices in matters of art flourish like weeds, whereas true ideals survive only by tireless cultivation. Success and popularity, even though deserved, produce a reaction. He lived long enough to know there was a new generation to whom he and his music were already old fashioned. His public were still faithful, but he could read the signs. The next outburst of German music would be no carrying on of his work but in some sort a protest against it.

For him music was song. He made the orchestra sing, he made the piano sing, he wanted to make his people sing, great choruses of people, human voices joining the voices of all instruments. Bach with his choir in the old Leipzig church had shown the way. For a moment he had believed the *Singakademie* would carry on. But only in England had he found a general love of music in this large and noble form, numerous groups of men and women, the men, all amateurs, who liked to sing well. Germany would produce great professionals, but the people at large would listen—and criticize.

To make the slightest observation which would qualify Mendelssohn's happiness in his family may seem both ungracious and unnecessary, yet without implying any disparagement of the devoted wife whom he loved devotedly, we notice the fact that in his own home he alone supplied the intellectual and creative atmosphere which in his father's house had been the contribution of every member of the circle. Now that his parents were gone, it was to his sisters and his brother Paul that he turned to discuss his chief interests. His constant traveling, with inevitable separations from his wife and his children, he speaks of as a sacrifice to his art, and whenever he could he made up for these intervals by brief vacations, periods of concentrated domesticity, but if there was time for a trip to Switzerland or to whatever rest resort, he would be joined by Paul or by other relatives. It is to his wife's credit that she let him be happy in his own way, but she and he must have known his craving for a companionship which she could not entirely give. She may or may not have known that beyond the affection which he poured out on those of his flesh and blood, music was his only love.

Some biographers have raised the question whether there was not in the Mendelssohn family some inherited weakness which would explain his early death. Since his grandfather and his father lived out a reasonable span, the hypothesis is not impressive. Some who are inclined to rate his work not too high, suggest that he might have done better if he had tried to excel in fewer directions, that he might have lived longer if he hadn't tried to do so much. But who is to say that a longer life would have meant more to him or to us? We have commented on the tragic undertone of his last years merely to define his genius; only for the same purpose do we recall here the opinion that he spread himself too thin. He was one type of artist; if you prefer the other kind, then you prefer it, but both kinds will continue to appear unless nature changes her habit.

164

Plato believed in the kind of artist who limits himself. No man, he told us, can expect to succeed in more than one art. On the other hand Michelangelo and Leonardo da Vinci did quite well in several directions. However Mendelssohn may rank beneath them in final accomplishment, he belongs to their kind; he was of the type in whom the creative impulse is joined to insatiable curiosity. He was a musician, but he must learn how to paint, he must give precious time to translating poetry and composing verses of his own, he must think out new methods of education. It was his temperament; he had no choice. None of the explorers in art was ever quite happy, except during early youth when the extent of the quest is not yet known and there still seems to be time enough. More than one adventurous spirit, aware at last that there must be an end, has thrown himself into a final work curiously related to the achievements with which his career began. Mendelssohn's first important triumph was the revival of the *St. Matthew Passion;* his last was *Elijah.*

His general activities, of course, were not greatly curtailed, but little by little he began to save himself for what was most urgent. We can imagine his regret at missing the first performance of his Violin Concerto, when his friend David played it gloriously in Leipzig on March 18, 1845. At the moment, however, he felt too exhausted to spend his energies on work already done; the Concerto was secure, the oratorio must be finished.

He had put together the text with the help of Pastor Schubring, a very remarkable text indeed, which repays examination. By May, 1846, the first part of the score was complete and a good portion of the second part. In a fury of composition he got the whole work ready for performance on August 26, 1846, at Birmingham. It was his ninth visit to England, the climax of all the visits, perhaps of his entire life. The music was beautifully rendered. "Nothing of mine," he said, "ever went so well at the first performance, or was greeted so enthusiastically by the musicians and the public." Later audiences have agreed with the earliest, that this oratorio shares the front rank with Handel's *Messiah,* and that in some ways it is the most exciting of all oratorios. Singers are likely to praise it still more highly.

It has the advantage of an extraordinary libretto. The story of Elijah provided episodes not usually found in such a text, strong situations with an elementary or primitive or at times barbaric appeal, conflict of rival faiths, moods of despair and of triumph, the prophet and his people sometimes at odds, the will of Jehovah made clear only after seasons of doubt. The famine and drought, the duel with the priests of Baal and the unrestrained delight in their destruction, the drama of the landscape and the weather, the whirlwind, fire, mountains, valleys, hot suns, night and cool stars—Mendelssohn brings them all before us through music which for descriptive power has never been excelled. His canvas is as heroic as the ceiling of the Sistine Chapel, and the conception of the prophet Elijah in largeness, in mystery and in dignity, might have sprung from Michelangelo's imagination. The gods of Richard Wagner's Valhalla are in comparison lethargic and garrulous.

The first part of the libretto, as it were the first act, deals with Elijah's triumphs over the drought and over the priests of Baal. Quite unconventionally the drama is outlined at once in the prophet's recitative telling us that no more rain is to fall. The magnificent overture which immediately follows is supposed to describe the drought, and even if you are one of those who hold that music can portray nothing to the eye, you will probably agree that sound can provoke the imagination, and in this instance you undoubtedly will feel the sufferings of a whole people. The effect upon the hearer is of a mounting intensity, a cumulation of nervous excitement, until the opening chorus breaks out in the cry, "Help, Lord!"

In my boyhood when I first heard *Elijah* this chorus seemed to bring into the concert hall the victims themselves, pleading for rescue—or rather, the concert hall disappeared, the parched landscape took its place, and the voices were of a primitive folk uttering the universal and eternal prayer for food. I was astonished then, as many another has been before and since, that an oratorio could be dramatic as well as lyrical, and still more that Mendelssohn, of all composers, should have presented the drama in such elemental terms. You may say that the elemental quality was already present in the Biblical story of the heroic prophet, and this of course is true, but few of us recognize that quality in full till Mendelssohn makes it clear for us.

Compare this opening chorus with the beginning of Handel's *Messiah*, the noble recitative, "Comfort ye my people." The idea in both cases is the same, mortal need and divine salvation. In the *Messiah*, however, the people are sung about, whereas in *Elijah* they speak for themselves. And there is this more profound difference, that in the *Messiah* the need and the rescue are interpreted, by both music and text, on spiritual heights, but in *Elijah* on a very human level, close to earth, with water and fire among the chief actors, with the weather always important, as well as the time of day or night. In this domain of nature we meet passions not only elemental but primitive, fear and hate as well as faith, hope and charity. Here is something very different from the *Hymn of Praise* or *St. Paul*, a startling work to come from the composer of *Midsummer Night's Dream*, yet so characteristic of Mendelssohn that if he had died before its completion we should not have known his genius in its essence.

The modern composer, like the modern artist in all mediums, is inclined to be an egotist or at least a strong individual. Chopin may or may not have put into his masterpieces the grief of Poland, but primarily he was expressing his own temperament; Richard Wagner may have wished to compose some kind of folk epic for his country, and his country may or may not care to recognize itself in the curious domestic entanglements of the *Ring,* but the world in general accepts the result as the very personal contribution of Richard Wagner, a series of longish operas, without dancing, sometimes repetitious, at other times majestically and poignantly inspired. But from his youth Mendelssohn, virtuoso though he was, dreamt of a musical development in which the chorus, the folk voice, should have the chief role. If Bach taught him the principle, the example of Greek tragedy suggested a still more dramatic application. The *Elijah* is the fruitful result, in itself worth while and indicating, as other great oratorios do not, still further developments.

The chorus here, we should notice, expresses the emotions of mankind in general faced with various crises and swayed always by the forces of the moment. In the Mendelssohnian chorus, however, we need not expect to find abstract moral principles nor even a complete statement of religious faith. The prophet Elijah is represented, for all his nobleness of character, as an individual, very human; his task is to wrestle with titanic forces—with nature, with evil, with the frailty and the stupidity of mankind in the crowd. Eternal principles are stated by small groups of voices, angelic choirs, or in the solos assigned to tenor, contralto, soprano. There are also one or two serene choruses, of the kind we have met already in *St. Paul* and the *Hymn of Praise,* but the effect of them is not primarily choral; they might just as well be sung by a quartet or a double quartet. In general it can be said that the large body of voices is used to state the universal attitudes of humanity.

The illustrations of these remarks are found in the next numbers. The lovely duet, "Zion spreadeth her hands," is accompanied by the prayer of the people, "Lord, bow Thine ear," a remarkable blending of narrative with lyrical elements. The tenor recitative, "Ye people, rend your hearts," and the well-known solo, "If with all your hearts," state the terms of the gathering drama in which the prophet will need encouragement not only against the priests of Baal but also against the despair of his own people. In the following numbers we hear the summons to the test, we feel the loneliness of the prophet as he answers the call, we understand the source of his strength in the double quartet for sopranos and altos, "For He shall give His angels," and in the serene chorus, "Blessed are the men." This chorus is fairly familiar, since its beauty tempts many a church choirmaster to try it, even with forces not quite capable of sustaining its long phrases, but the double quartet is rarely heard outside of the concert hall, and not always satisfactorily heard there, few conductors having at their command eight well-matched voices. But where all the conditions are right this number is one of the finest in any oratorio. The music moves briskly, yet the mood induced is peaceful, faith-strengthening, angelic.

With the powerful recitative, "As God the Lord liveth," the duel between Jehovah and Baal begins, the prayers of Israel alternating with prayers of the Baal priests, Israel gaining confidence, the Baal priests growing frantic, until the moment comes for Elijah to call the fire from heaven. Does his own faith waver a little? He pauses for a telling moment, pours his heart out in the deeply-moving prayer, "Lord God of Abraham," finds comfort in the answering quartet, "Cast thy burden upon the Lord," and with sudden resolution gives the command for the divine wrath to fall.

The triumphant chorus, "The fire descends from heaven," is always immensely satisfying to the audience, who at the close of this nerve-rousing sequence have little pity for the priests of Baal and can therefore enjoy seeing them all slain. Whatever primitive angers are roused by a battle to the death, Mendelssohn here expresses without reserve. Jehovah is vindicated, and the pack is in at the kill.

After such a climax a lesser genius might have left half-finished the theme of the drought, the major affliction which has fallen on the people because of their imperfect faith. Mendelssohn presents the Baal episode, however, not as the occasion merely for renewed trust in the prophet, but as a lesson for the people in their relation to Jehovah, a lesson in humility and obedience. From the mood of primitive triumph, in the furious bass solo, "Is not His word like a fire," we pass directly to the higher insight, the spiritual warning against conceit and self-sufficiency, in the contralto air, "Woe unto them who forsake Him." Immediately afterwards we hear the long petition for rain, this time the prophet and the people in complete accord. The rain comes, and the first half of the oratorio closes in the chorus, "Thanks be to God," as triumphant an utterance as music is likely ever to give us.

The second part of the oratorio is sometimes said to be

less dramatic than the first, but whether we agree with that opinion depends on a definition. The music of the second part is probably more majestic and in places more exciting than anything in the early section, but the drama is no longer primitive; it is not even external; it is the conflict within a great soul, far too great for his time. Elijah is satisfied with nothing that he has accomplished; the success with which he has served the people leaves him not at all at peace with the universe but weary of life; goodness in the moment of weariness seems not its own reward but a thankless and never-finished discipline. For Mendelssohn to make so much of his theme is very revealing. The supreme talents who have followed their bent and have won what the rest of us would think are the rich rewards, end more often than not in melancholy at last, desiring no other life than the one they have led but questioning its meaning. The prophet in the second part of the oratorio is not simply a notable religious leader, not simply the inspired sage, the teacher of his people; he seems rather the symbol of all greatness, lonely in his gifts and baffled by his own privileges. The second half of the oratorio is filled with comfort for just that kind of discouragement. Elijah, low in spirit, asks for death: "It is enough; now Lord take away my life." The answer is stressed in the trio, "Lift thine eyes," in the contralto solo, "O rest in the Lord," in the two choruses, "He watching over Israel," and "He that shall endure till the end." In some performances omissions are made in this sequence, precisely because the central idea of assured faith is repeated a bit more than seems necessary, but this repetition is important for its disclosure of the inner Mendelssohn. Or so some of us believe.

The chorus, "Behold, God the Lord passed by," introduces the final section of the oratorio, a nobly eloquent section, full of gorgeous passages and of isolated phrases, as in the very last page, where the tenors suggest not only a confident faith but an indescribable longing. Why this emphasis on aspiration, on something unfinished, perhaps unattainable?

There have been critics who found a racial explanation for the peculiar greatness of *Elijah*. They have thought that Mendelssohn at the end of his work was speaking for the race from which he came, expressing in the character of the prophet a dedication to an ideal which has not been attained in history and which has encountered tragic opposition. This hypothesis may be true, but it rests on no evidence and perhaps it makes Mendelssohn a far narrower man than he was. Without regard to race, most audiences hearing this unusual music understand the broadly human truths which sufficiently explain its underlying sadness and yearning. If any further guess must be made, perhaps it is enough to suppose that Mendelssohn was consciously or unconsciously summing up his own life. He had come a long way in a few miraculous years, he had given his generation music which still is loved throughout the world, but he had set for himself a measure of perfection and he knew the difference between the hope and the fulfilment.

173

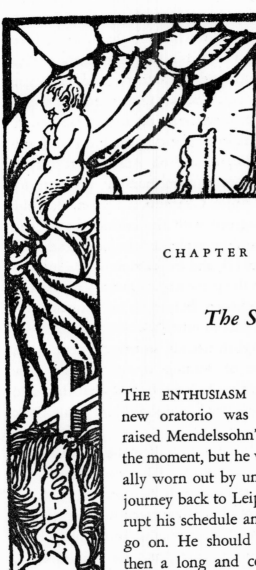

CHAPTER FIFTEEN

The Silence

THE ENTHUSIASM WITH WHICH THE new oratorio was hailed in England raised Mendelssohn's spirits, at least for the moment, but he was a sick man, literally worn out by unsparing toil. On his journey back to Leipzig he had to interrupt his schedule and gather strength to go on. He should have given himself then a long and complete rest, but as usual the performance had suggested revisions, and he continued to work on the text until it was finally published in June, 1847. At the same time he responded to demands from which he should have been spared. For the King of Prussia he composed a setting of the German liturgy and an anthem, and he began *Christus,* an oratorio which he left unfinished and which would probably have added nothing to his reputation. In April, 1847, he was in England again for a performance of the revised *Elijah,* and on April 26 at a Philharmonic concert he gave a memorable performance of the Beethoven G major Concerto, a lifelong favorite of his. He himself agreed with the critics that he had never played better, and he explained the superb achievement in spite of overwork and exhaustion by the inspiration he received from the presence of Queen Victoria and Jenny Lind in the audience. Before he left England for the last time he took part in other concerts, but his work was done, and his English friends, grieving a little at his prodigal expenditure of waning strength, knew they would not see him again. At least, that is what they said afterwards, though few tried to restrain him while there was yet time.

When he returned to the Continent he was plunged into grief by the sudden death of his sister Fanny, his beloved companion. A summer in Switzerland with his family failed to restore him. Some compositions, not important, belong to the closing months. In October, back in Leipzig, he suffered a stroke, and on November 4, 1847, he died.

The funeral took place in the Pauliner Church, Leipzig. During the service the chorus "Happy and blest" from *St. Paul* was sung, and the concluding chorus from Bach's *St. Matthew Passion*. The body was taken to Berlin and buried in the Trinity Churchyard, near the Halle Gate.

A lovable man, a noble life, an enduring fame. After such popularity as his a reaction was inevitable, and the titanic figure of Wagner for a while cast him into the shade. Ears tuned to rich modern harmonies find him old-fashioned and simple. But Schubert and Haydn, even Mozart, went through their period of undervaluing, and Mendelssohn begins to come once more to his own. He seems to the judicious and expert a master still among the great composers for the orchestra, an unsurpassed handler of large choral effects, an inexhaustible source of pure song—and best of all, perhaps, one of the complete lovers of beauty who in their lives as well as their works gave to the art of music a new dedication and a nobler dignity.

LIST OF MENDELSSOHN'S WORKS

List of Mendelssohn's Works

Taken from the Thematic Catalogue published by Messrs. Breitkopf and Hartel, 1822, with additions and corrections from other sources, by Sir George Grove in his *Dictionary of Music and Musicians*. Quoted here by permission of the Macmillan Company, Publishers.

OPUS	TITLE	DATE OF COMPOSITION
1.	Quartet in C minor, No. 1, pf. and strings.	*Begun,* Secheron, Sept. 20, 1822. *Ended,* Berlin, Oct. 18, 1922.
2.	Do. in F minor, No. 2.	Nov. 19 and 30; Dec. 3, 1823.
3.	Do. in B minor, No. 3.	Oct. 7, 1824; Jan. 3, 1825—*at end,* Jan. 18, 1825.
4.	Sonata, in F minor, pf. and vn.	
5.	Capriccio, in F sharp minor, pf.	Berlin, July 23, 1825.
6.	Sonata, in E, pf.	Berlin, March 22, 1826.
7.	Seven characteristic pieces, pf.	
8.	12 Songs (No. 12 duet). *N.B.* —Nos. 2, 3, and 12 are by Fanny Mendelssohn-Bartholdy.	
9.	12 Songs (Part I, The Youth; Part II, The Maiden). *N.B.* —Nos. 7, 10, and 12 are by Fanny Mendelssohn-Bartholdy.	No. 3, Berlin, April 3, 1829 (?).
10.	*The Wedding of Camacho,* comic opera in 2 acts.	*At the end,* Berlin, August 10, 1825.
11.	Symphony in C minor, No. 1, *Sinfonia xiii in* C, orch.	March 3, 9, 31, 1824.
12.	Quartet in E flat, No. 1, strings.	London, Sept. 14, 1829.
13.	Do. in A, No. 2.	Berlin, Oct. 26, 1827.

14. Rondo capriccioso in E, pf.
15. Fantasie in E, pf. On the Irish air, *The Last Rose of Summer.*
16. 3 Fantasies (or Caprices) in A minor, E minor, and E major, pf.   No. 1, Coed-du, North Wales, Sept. 4, 1829, *Rosen und Nelken in Menge;* No. 2, Norwood, Surrey, Nov. 13, 1829; No. 3, Coed-du, Sept. 5, 1829.
17. Variations concertantes in D, pf. and violoncello.   Berlin, Jan. 30, 1829.
18. Quintet in A, strings.   *Andante,* "Nachruf," Paris, Sept. 23, 1831.
19. 6 Songs, voice and pf.
    6 Songs without words, Book I, Original English title: *Melodies for the pianoforte.*   No. 6, "Auf einer Gondel," Venice, Oct. 16, 1830.
20. Octet in E flat, strings.
21. *A Midsummer Night's Dream,* Concert overture, in E, No. 1, orch.   Berlin, August 6, 1826.
22. Capriccio brillante in B minor, pf. and orch.
23. 3 Pieces of Church music, solo, chorus, and organ:—
    No. 1, *Aus tiefer Noth (In deep distress).*
    No. 2, *Ave Maria* (8 voices).
    No. 3, *Mitten wir* (8 voices).
24. Overture in C, Wind band, *für Harmoniemusik.*
25. Concerto in G minor, pf. and orch., No. 1.
26. *The Hebrides,* or *Fingal's Cave,* Concert overture in B minor, No. 2, orch.   First form, Rome, Dec. 16, 1830; revised form, London, June 20, 1832.
27. Calm sea and prosperous voy-

age, Concert overture, in D,
No. 3, orch.

28.	Fantasie in F sharp minor, *Sonate Ecossaise*, pf.	Berlin, Jan. 29, 1833.
29.	Rondo (or Capriccio) brillante in E flat, pf. and orch.	Düsseldorf, Jan. 29, 1834.
30.	6 Songs without words, pf., Book II, English titles: *Six Melodies* and *Six Romances*.	No. 4, Jan. 30, 1833 (?). No. 5, Dec. 12, 1833.
31.	Psalm 115, chorus and orch., *Not unto us, O Lord.*	Nov. 15, 1830.
32.	*To the story of the lovely Melusina*, Concert Overture in F, No. 4, orch.	Düsseldorf, Nov. 14, 1833.
33.	3 Caprices in A minor, E, B flat minor, pf.	No. 1, April 9, 1834; No. 3, London, July 25, 1833.
34.	6 Songs, voice and pf.	No. 1, Düsseldorf, May 11, 1834; No. 5, Dec. 28, 1834.
35.	6 Preludes and Fugues, pf.	No. 2, Prel., Leipzig, Dec. 6-8, 1836; No. 3, Fugue, Berlin, Sept. 21, 1832; No. 4, Fugue, Düsseldorf, Jan. 6, 1835; No. 5, Prel., Leipzig, Nov. 19, 1836; Fugue, Düsseldorf, Dec. 3, 1834; No. 6, Prel., Leipzig, Jan. 3, 1837; Fugue, Nov. 27, 1836.
36.	*St. Paul*, oratorio.	Part I, Leipzig, April 8, 1836; Part II, Leipzig, April 18, 1836.
37.	3 Preludes and Fugues, organ.	No. 1, Prel., Spires, April 2, 1837; No. 2, Prel., Spires, April 4, 1837; Fugue, Leipzig, Dec. 1, 1837; No. 3, Prel., Spires, April 6, 1837.

38.	6 Songs without words, pf., Book III.	No. 5, Spires, April 6, 1837; No. 6, Duet, Frankfort, June 27, 1836.
39.	3 Motets, female voices and organ (or pf.) *Für die Stimmen der Nonnen auf Sta-Trinita de' Monti.*	Rome, Dec. 31, 1830. Another version of "Surrexit Pastor," headed "No. 2," in the MS., is dated "Coblentz, August 14, 1837."
40.	Concerto in D minor, pf. and orch., No. 2.	Horchheim, August 5, 1837.
41.	6 Part-songs, S.A.T.B., "for singing in the open air," 1st set. The earliest appearance of Mendelssohn's Four-part songs in England was in No. 55 of Ewer & Co.'s Orpheus collection, which began in 1836.	No. 4, Düsseldorf, Jan. 22, 1834.
42.	Psalm 42, soli, chorus, and orch., *As the hart pants.*	
43.	Serenade and Allegro giojoso in B minor, pf. and orch.	April 11, 1838.
44.	3 Quartets in D, E minor, E flat, strings, Nos. 3, 4, and 5.	No. 3, Berlin, July 24, 1838; No. 4, June 18, 1837; No. 5, Feb. 6, 1838.
45.	Sonata in B flat, pf. and violoncello.	Leipzig, Oct. 13, 1838.
46.	Psalm 95, tenor solo, chorus, and orch., *O come let us worship.*	Final chorus (in E flat), Leipzig, April 11, 1839.
47.	6 Songs, voice and pf.	No. 3, Leipzig, April 17, 1839; No. 4, April 18, 1839; No. 5, London, May 1832.
48.	6 Part-Songs, S.A.T.B., 2nd set.	No. 1, July 5 [1839]; No. 3, Leipzig, Dec. 28, 1839; No. 4, June 15 [1839];

49. Trio in D minor, pf., violin and violoncello.

No. 5, Nov. 18, 1839; No. 6, Leipzig, Dec. 26, 1839. *Allegro,* Frankfort, June 6, 1839; *Finale,* Frankfort, July 18, 1839; and Leipzig, Sept. 23, 1839.

50. 6 Part-songs, male voices.

No. 2, *Der Jager Abschied,* with wind accompaniments, Leipzig, Jan. 6, 1840; No. 5, Dec. 7, 1839; No. 6, Jan. 6, 1840.

51. Psalm 114, 8-part chorus and orch., *When Israel out of Egypt came.*

Horchheim, Aug. 9, 1839.

52. Lobgesang (Hymn of Praise), Symphony-cantata.

Leipzig, Nov. 27, 1840 (revised form).

53. 6 Songs without words, pf., Book IV.

No. 5, April 30, 1841; No. 6, May 1, 1841.

54. 17 Variations Sérieuses in D minor, pf.

June 4, 1841.

55. Antigone of Sophocles; music to, male voices and orch.

Berlin, Oct. 10, 1841.

56. Symphony in A minor, *The Scotch,* No. 3, orch.

Berlin, Jan. 20, 1842.

57. 6 Songs, voice and pf.

No. 2, April 20, 1839 (*cf.* op. 88, No. 3); No. 5 *Rendez-vous,* Berlin, Oct. 17, 1842; No. 6, *Frische Fahrt,* April 29, 1841.

58. Sonata in D, pf. and violoncello, No. 2.

59. 6 Part-songs, S.A.T.B., 3rd set.

No. 1, Leipzig, Nov. 23, 1837; No. 2, Jan. 17, 1843; No. 3, Leipzig, March 4, 1843; No. 4, Leipzig, June 19, 1843; No. 5, March 4, 1843; No. 6, *Vorüber,* March 5, 1843.

60. First Walpurgis night, Music to Goethe's *Ballad,* chorus and orch.

1st version, Milan, July 15, 1831, and Paris, Feb. 13, 1832.

61. *A Midsummer Night's Dream,* Music to, solo, chorus, and orch. (exclusive of overture, for which see op. 21).

62. 6 Songs without words, pf., Book V.

No. 1, Jan. 6 and 12, 1844; No. 2, July 29, 1843; No. 6, Denmark Hill, June 1, 1842.

63. 6 Duets, voices and pf.

No. 1, Frankfort, Dec. 1836; No. 4 originally for pf. duet; No. 5, Berlin, Oct. 17, 1842; No. 6, Jan. 23, 1844.

64. Concerto in E, vn. and orch.

Sept. 16, 1844.

65. 6 Sonatas, organ. [For the history of these organ sonatas, see *Musical Times,* 1901, p. 794, and 1906, p. 95.]

Son. 1: No. 1, Frankfort, Dec. 28, 1844; No. 2, Dec. 19, 1844; No. 4, Aug. 18, 1844.

Son. 2: No. 1, Frankfort, Dec. 21, 1844; No. 3 (Fugue), July 14, 1839, and Dec. 19, 1844.

Son. 3: No. 1, August 9, 1844; No. 2, Aug. 17, 1844.

Son. 4: Nos. 1 and 2, Frankfort, Jan. 2, 1845.

Son. 5: Nos. 2 and 3, Sept. 9, 1844.

Son. 6: No. 1, Frankfort, Jan. 26, 1845; No. 4 (Fugue), Frankfort, Jan. 27, 1845.

66. Trio in C minor, pf., vn., and violoncello.

67. 6 Songs without words, pf. (Book VI). — No. 1, June 29, 1843; No. 2, Frankfort, May 3, 1845; No. 5, Jan. 5 and 12, 1844.

68. *An die Künstler (To the sons of art)*. Schiller's poem, Festgesang. Male voices and brass instruments. Composed for the opening of the first German-Flemish vocal festival at Cologne, June, 1846.

69. 3 English Church pieces, solo voices and chorus—(1) Nunc dimittis; (2) Jubilate; (3) Magnificat. — No. 1, Baden-Baden, June 12, 1847; No. 2, Leipzig, April 5, 1847; No. 3, Baden-Baden, June 12, 1847.

70. *Elijah*, oratorio. — *At the end,* Leipzig, Aug. 11, 1846.

71. 6 Songs, voice and pf. — No. 1, Leipzig, Dec. 22, 1845; No. 2, Frankfort, April 3, 1845; No. 3, Leipzig, Sept. 22, 1847; No. 4, Berlin, Nov. 3, 1842; No. 5, Interlaken, July 27, 1847; No. 6, Oct. 1, 1847.

72. 6 Kinderstücke, pf. Known in England as *Christmas pieces* and composed at Denmark Hill, London. — No. 1, June 24, 1842; No. 3, June 21, 1842.

FROM OP. 73 TO OP. 121 ARE POSTHUMOUS WORKS

73. Lauda Sion, cantata, chorus and orch. For St. Martin's church, Liège. — Feb. 10, 1846.

74. *Athalie,* Music to Racine's, soli, chorus, and orch. — Choruses, Leipzig, July 4, 1843; Overture, London, June 13, 1844; and Berlin, Nov. 12, 1845.

75. 4 Part-songs, male voices. — No. 1, Feb. 8, 1844; No. 2, Nov. 14, 1839.

76.	4 Part-songs, male voices.	No. 2, Feb. 9, 1844; No. 3, Leipzig, Oct. 8, 1846.
77.	3 duets, voices and pf. No. 3 is from *Ruy Blas*.	No. 1, Leipzig, Dec. 3, 1836; No. 2, Leipzig, Jan. 18, 1847; No. 3, Leipzig, Feb. 14, 1839.
78.	3 Psalms—the 2nd, 43rd, and 22nd, solo and chorus. For the Domchor, Berlin.	No. 2, Berlin, Jan. 17, 1844.
79.	6 Anthems, 8-part chorus. For the Domchor, Berlin.	No. 2, Berlin, Dec. 25, 1843; No. 4, Feb. 14, 1844; No. 5, Oct. 5, 1846; No. 6, Feb. 18, 1844.
80.	Quartet in F minor, strings.	Interlaken, Sept., 1847.
81.	Andante in E, Scherzo in A minor, Capriccio in E minor, Fugue in E flat, strings.	
82.	Variations in E flat, pf.	Leipzig, July 25, 1841.
83a.	Variations in B flat, pf.	
83b.	Variations arranged for 4 hands.	
84.	3 Songs for a low voice and pf.	No. 1, Düsseldorf, Dec. 5, 1831; No. 2, Feb. 26, 1839; No. 3, May 25, 1834.
85.	6 Songs without words, pf., Book VII.	No. 2, Düsseldorf, June 9, 1834; No. 4, Frankfort, May 3 and 6, 1845; No. 5, Frankfort, May 7, 1845; No. 6, May 1, 1841.
86.	6 Songs, voice and pf.	No. 3, Unterseen, August 10, 1831; No. 6, Oct. 7, 1847.
87.	Quintet in B flat, strings.	Soden, July 8, 1845.
88.	6 Part-songs, S.A.T.B., (4th set).	No. 1, Aug. 8, 1844; No. 2, Leipzig, June 20, 1843; No. 3, April 20, 1839; No. 4, Leipzig, June 19, 1843; No. 6, Leipzig, March 10, 1840.

89. Heimkehr aus der Fremde *(Son and Stranger)*, Singspiel in 1 Act.

90. The Italian Symphony, Symphony in A, orch. Berlin, March 13, 1833.

91. Psalm 98, *Sing to the Lord,* 8-part chorus and orch. For the Festival Service in Berlin Cathedral on New Year's Day, 1844. Dec. 27, 1843.

92. Allegro brillante in A, pf., 4 hands. Leipzig, March 23, 1841.

93. Oedipus in Colonos by Sophocles, Music to, male voices and orch. Frankfort, Feb. 25, 1845.

94. *Infelice!* Concert-air in B flat, soprano solo and orch. 1st version, with vn. obbl., April 3, 1834; 2nd version, Leipzig, Jan. 15, 1843.

95. *Ruy Blas,* Overture, orch. Leipzig, March 8, 1839.

96. Hymn, alto solo, chorus and orch. Composed for Mr. [Dr.] C. Broadley. Leipzig, Dec. 14, 1840; Jan. 5, 1843 (final chorus). Autograph in British Museum (Add. MS. 31,801).

97. Christus, unfinished oratorio. Recitatives and choruses.

98. (1) Lorelei, unfinished opera, solo, chorus, and orch. Finale to 1st act.
(2) Lorelei, Ave Maria, solo and chorus of female voices.
(3) Lorelei. Vintage chorus, male voices and orch.

99. 6 Songs, voice and pf. No. 1, Berlin, Aug. 9, 1841; No. 4, June 6, 1841; No. 5, Leipzig, Dec. 22, 1845.

100. 4 Part-songs, S.A.T.B. No. 1, Aug. 8, 1844; No. 2, June 20, 1843; No. 4, Frankfort, June 14, 1839.

101. Overture in C *(Trumpet overture)*, orch.

102. 6 Songs without words, pf., Book VIII.

No. 1, London, June 1, 1842; No. 2, Frankfort, May 11, 1845; Pfingsten; Nos. 3 and 5 (Kinderstück), Dec. 12, 1845.

103. Trauer-Marsch in A minor, orch. For funeral of Norbert Burgmüller.

104. 3 Preludes and 3 Studies, pf. (2 parts).

Bk. 1, No. 1, Leipzig, Dec. 8, 1836; No. 2, Oct. 12, 1836; No. 3, Nov. 27, 1836.
Bk. 2, No. 1, June 9, 1836; No. 2, Düsseldorf, April 21, 1834.

105. Sonata in G minor, pf.

Begun, June 16, 1820. *Presto,* August 18, 1821.

106. Sonata in B flat, pf.

Berlin, May 31, 1827.

107. *The Reformation Symphony in D, No. 5,* orch.

108. March in D, orch. For the fête given to the painter, Cornelius, at Dresden in April, 1841.

109. Song without words in D, violoncello and pf.

110. Sextet in D, pf., vn., 2 violas, violoncello and bass.

April and May, 1824.

111. Tu es Petrus, 5-part chorus and orch.

Nov., 1827.

112. 2 Sacred songs, voice and pf. (No. 2, composed originally for *St. Paul*).

113 & 114. 2 Concerted pieces, clarinet and basset-horn, with pf. accompt., in F major and D minor.

No. 1, Berlin, Jan. 19, 1833.

115.	2 Sacred choruses, male voices.	
116.	Funeral song, mixed voices.	Soden, July 8, 1845.
117.	Album - Blatt, song without words in E minor, pf.	
118.	Capriccio in E, pf.	Bingen, July 11, 1837.
119.	Perpetuum mobile in C, pf.	
120.	4 Part-songs, male voices.	No. 2, Leipzig, Feb. 20, 1847.
121.	Responsorium et Hymnus, male voices, with accompt. of violoncello and bass (organ).	

WORKS WITHOUT OPUS NUMBERS

TITLE	DATE OF COMPOSITION
Etude in F minor, pf. For the *Méthode des Méthodes.*	Leipzig, March 13, 1836.
Scherzo in B minor, pf.	
Scherzo and Capriccio in F sharp minor, pf. For the Pianist's Album.	
2 Romances of Lord Byron's, voice and pf.: *There be none of beauty's daughters,* and *Sun of the sleepless.*	No. 2, Düsseldorf, Dec. 31, 1834.
Verleih' uns Frieden; Grant us Thy peace, Prayer, chorus and orch.	Rome, Feb. 10, 1831.
Andante cantabile and Presto agitato in B, pf. For the Album of 1839.	Berlin, June 22, 1838.
The Garland, voice and pf., poem by Thomas Moore.	London, May 24, 1829.
Ersatz für Unbestand, part-song, male voices, poem by Rückert. For Tauchnitz's Musenalmanach.	Nov. 22, 1839.
Festgesang, male chorus and orch. Composed for the Gutenberg Festival at Leipzig, held in 1840, in celebration of the invention of printing. [No. 2 is associated in England with the words of Charles Wesley's Christmas hymn *Hark! the herald angels sing,* to which it was adapted by Dr. W. H. Cummings.]	

Gondellied in A, pf. *Auf einer Gondel.*	Leipzig, Feb. 5, 1837.
3 Volkslieder, 2 voices and pf.	
Lord, have mercy upon us (Kyrie). *For evening service.* Voices only. *For Mr. Attwood.* In the *Album für Gesang.* First published in England in Ewer's Orpheus, Book XII.	Berlin, March 24, 1833.
Prelude and fugue in E minor, pf. For the Album Notre temps.	Prelude, Leipzig, July 13, 1841; Fugue, June 16, 1827.
3 Sacred choruses, forming part of op. 96.	Leipzig, Jan. 5, 1843.
Hear my prayer, hymn, soprano solo, chorus, and organ; afterwards orchestrated, the full score is only published in England, not in Germany.	Jan. 25, 1844.
Warnung vor dem Rhein, poem by C. Simrock, voice and pf.	
2 Songs, voice and pf.	No. 1, Berlin, August 17, 1835.
2 Songs, voice and pf.	No. 1, April 20, 1841.
2 Clavierstücke, in B flat and G minor, pf.	
Seemann's Scheidelied, poem by Hoffmann v. Fallersleben, voice and pf.	
Nachtgesang, 4 male voices.	Berlin, Jan. 15, 1842.
Die Stiftungsfeier, 4 male voices. *Für die Stiftungsfeier der Gesellschaft der Freunde in Berlin,* Jan., 1842.	
Des Mädchens Klage, Romance, voice and pf.	
Kyrie Eleison, mixed voices, double chorus (Deutsche Liturgie).	Oct. 28, 1846.
Ehre sei Gott in der Höhe; Heilig: Psalm 100. Three sacred pieces, Nos. 1 and 2, double choir; No. 3,	

4 voices, from *Musica Sacra,* Band
7, Nos. 17 and 18, No. 10.

Te Deum in A (English Church Service).

The Evening Bell, for harp and pf.   Norwood, Nov. 1829.
The "bell" was that of Attwood's
gate. See "Musical Haunts in London," p. 5.

Fugue in F minor, organ.   Frankfort, July 18, 1839.

Two pieces, organ.
    (1) Andante with variations in D.   July 23, 1844.
    (2) Allegro in B flat.   Dec. 31, 1844.

Duo concertant, variations upon the
March in Weber's Preciosa, pf., 4
hands, jointly composed by Mendelssohn and Ignaz Moscheles.

NOT INCLUDED IN THE THEMATIC CATALOGUE

[Hymn-tune, Psalm xxxi, *Defend me,*   Feb. 27, 1839.
Lord, from shame. Composed for
the "National Psalmist" (1839),
edited by Charles Danvers Hackett.]

Praeludium in C minor for the organ.   Leipzig, July 9, 1841.
Composed for Mr. Henry E. Dibdin.

Additional (final) chorus to Psalm 95   Leipzig, April 11, 1839.
(op. 46).

String quartet in E flat. Autograph in   March 5-30, 1823.
British Museum (Add. MS. 30,900).

COMPOSITIONS EDITED ETC. BY MENDELSSOHN

Handel's *Dettingen Te Deum,* with additional accompaniments. Score and parts. (Kistner.)

[Handel's *Israel in Egypt,* edited for the London Handel Society; Mendelssohn wrote a special organ part, and the edition was published by Cramer & Co. in June, 1846. For the interesting correspondence with G. A. Macfarren on the subject of this edition, see "Goethe and Mendelssohn," 2nd edition, 1874, p. 169 *et seq.*]

Handel's *Acis and Galatea*, with additional accompaniments. (Novello.)

J. S. Bach's Chaconne for violin, with pf. accompt. (Ewer.)

[J. S. Bach's *Organ compositions on Chorales (Psalm tunes)*, Organ Preludes, etc., 2 books. (Coventry & Hollier, 1845.)

J. S. Bach's *Eleven variations on the Chorale Sei gegrusset Jesu gütig* (All hail, good Jesus), edited from the original manuscript. (Coventry & Hollier.)]

The collection of autograph MSS. of Mendelssohn, now preserved in the Royal Library, Berlin, comprise the following unpublished compositions:

11 Symphonies for strings.
1 Symphony for full orchestra.
Many Fugues for strings.
Concertos for pf.; vn.; pf. and vn. with quartet accompaniment.
2 Concertos for 2 pianos and orch. Trio for pf. vn. and viola.
2 Sonatas for pf. and vn. (one dated 1838).
1 Sonata for pf. and viola.
1 do. for pf. and clarinet.
2 Sonatas for pf. solo.
Many studies, Fantasias (1 for 4 hands), Fugues, etc., for pf. solo.
Many Fugues for Organ.
5 Operas and music to Calderon's *Steadfast Prince*.
1 Secular and 3 sacred cantatas.
Many songs and vocal pieces.
Organ part to Handel's *Solomon*.

LIST OF MENDELSSOHN
RECORDINGS

List of Mendelssohn Recordings

Andante from 6th Sonata for Organ, E. Commette—*C*.

Ave Maria, op. 98, Berlin Philharmonic Chorus—*V*.

Calm Sea and Prosperous Voyage, op. 27, London Symphony Orch., Blech—*V*.

Canzonetta from E flat Quartet, op. 12, Lener Quartet—*C*. "Add-a-Part" with first violin part to be added by player—*C*.

Concerto, op. 64, in E minor for Violin, Menuhin and Colonne Orch., Enesco—*V*. Kreisler and London Phil., Ronald—*V*. Szigeti and Royal Phil., Beecham—*C*.

Concerto, op. 25, in G minor for Piano, Dorfman and London Symphony Orch., Goehr—*C*.

Elijah—complete, B.B.C. Chorus and Orch., Robinson—*C*.

Elijah—many selections including: "O rest in the Lord," Matzenauer—*C*. "He, watching over Israel," Mormon Tab. Choir—*V*. "Hear ye, Israel," Marsh—*V*.

Hark! the Herald Angels Sing, Trinity Choir—*V*. B.B.C. Chorus—*C*.

Hear My Prayer, Temple Church (London) Chorus—*V*.

Hebrides (Fingal's Cave) Overture, op. 26, B.B.C. Orchestra, Boult—*V*. Queen's Hall Orchestra, Beecham—*C*.

Hunting Song, op. 120, Harvard Glee Club—*V*.

Hymn of Praise, op. 52, "All men, all things," B.B.C. Chorus—*C*.

Midsummer Night's Dream: Overture - Scherzo - Nocturne - Wedding March, San Francisco Symphony Orch., Hertz—*V*. Overture and Wedding March, Boston "Pops" Orchestra, Fiedler—*V*. Scherzo, N. Y. Phil. Orch., Toscanini—*V*. Wedding March and Nocturne, London Phil. Orch., Beecham—*C*.

On Wings of Song, op. 34, Elizabeth Schumann—*V*. For Violin, Heifetz—*V*.

Quartet in E flat, op. 12, Budapest String Quartet—*V*.

Quartet in D, op. 44, Stradivarius String Quartet—*C*.

Ruy Blas Overture, op. 95, B.B.C. Orch.—*V*. London Phil. Orch., Beecham—*C*.

Scherzo from String Octet, op. 20, Boston "Pops" Orch., Fiedler—*V*. Minneapolis Symph. Orch., Mitropoulos—*C*.

Scherzo from E minor Quartet, op. 44, Lener Quartet—*C*. Scherzo and Andante, Poltronieri Quartet—*C*.

Song Without Words, op. 109, in D (original), Casals—*V*.

Songs Without Words, Nos. 3, 6, 12, 14, 18, 20, 22, 32, 47—K. V. Schnabel—*V*. Other Songs and Songs Without Words—*C* and *V*.

St. Paul—But the Lord is mindful, Schumann-Heink—*V*. O great is the depth, B.B.C. Chorus and Orch.—*C*.

Symphony No. 3 in A minor (Scotch), Rochester Philharmonic Orch., Iturbi—*V*. Royal Phil. Orch., Weingartner—*C*.

Symphony No. 4 in A major (Italian), Boston Symphony Orch., Koussevitzky—*V*. Halle Orchestra, Harty—*C*.

Symphony No. 5 (Reformation), Columbia Broadcasting Co. Orch., Barlow—*C*.

Variations Sérieuses, op. 54, Cortot—*V*.

War March of the Priests (from "Athalie" op. 74), Phil. Symph. Orch. of N. Y., Mengelberg—*V*.

BIBLIOGRAPHY

Bibliography

Bennett (J. R. Sterndale): The Life of William Sterndale
Bennett.

Berlioz (Hector): Autobiography.

Chorley (Henry Fothergill): Thirty Years' Musical Recollection.

Devrient (Eduard): Recollections of Felix Mendelssohn-Bartholdy, and His Letters to Me, London,
1869.

Dorn (Heinrich): Recollections of Felix Mendelssohn and His
Friends. London. Temple Bar, Feb. 1872.

Eckardt (Julius): Ferdinand David und die Familie Mendelssohn-Bartholdy, 1888.

Edwards (F. G.): History of Elijah.

Goethe (J. W.): Briefwechsel mit einem Kind. 1834.
Correspondence with Zelter.

Grove (Sir George): Article: "Mendelssohn." Dictionary of
Music and Musicians.

Heine (Heinrich): Collected Works; Memoirs.

Hensel (Sebastian): The Mendelssohn Family.

Hiller (Ferdinand): Letters and Recollections of Felix Mendelssohn-Bartholdy.

Kaufman (Schima): A Second Elijah.

Mendelssohn-Bartholdy (Felix): Letters from Italy and Switzerland.

Letters: 1833-1847.

Moscheles (Felix): Briefe von Felix Mendelssohn-Bartholdy an Ignaz und Charlotte Moscheles.

Schubring (Julius): Briefwechsel mit Felix Mendelssohn-Bartholdy.

Spohr (Louis): Autobiography.

INDEX

Index